BEST of
INDIA

BEST of INDIA

The Choicest Regional Recipes

sitangsu chakravarty

Food Photographs by Amit Dey
Illustrations by Rohit Kathuria

PEARSON
Education

ISBN 81-7758-173-2

First Impression, 2006

Published by Dorling Kindersley (India) Pvt. Ltd., licensees of Pearson Education in South Asia.

Head Office: 482, F.I.E., Patparganj, Delhi 110 092, India.
Registered Office: 14 Local Shopping Centre, Panchsheel Park, New Delhi 110 017, India.

Printed in India

With love to my son Angshuman (Babai),
my daughter Madhurima (Mumpa), and my son-in-law Kris.

acknowledgements

There are many people without whose support and enthusiasm this book would not have seen the light of day. I wish to thank:

KPR Nair, who has been instrumental in publishing this book.

Amit Dey, for bringing the dishes to life with his excellent photography.

Ritu Singh, for editing the manuscript.

Friends and family, for their constant encouragement and support.

Finally, my wife Sujata, who has been a tremendous help, typing and retyping the manuscript, day and night in addition to her own job commitment.

Thank you, all.

Sitangsu

contents

snacks

vegetables

rice and bread

desserts

introduction

That variety is the spice of life is truly manifested in India, a country with a recorded history of 3,000 years, over 30 states, a host of languages spoken by its people and diversity in landscape—from snowy Kashmir to coastal Kerala, from the deserts of Rajasthan to the tea gardens of Assam.

The cuisine in India also varies tremendously from region to region, individual to individual, season to season, and occasion to occasion. Indian cooking is an art with a touch of science. The recipes in this book have been culled from my experience in different states during my career. While I do not claim to the authenticity of all the recipes, I have tried to maintain a good balance between the known, popular dishes and some unexplored regional ones.

During my long stay overseas in the course of my career I saw many Indian housewives shy away from exploring the popular dishes of their region. I have written this book keeping in mind working couples who have no time for elaborate cooking due to their hectic lifestyle, and those who are curious to learn various regional cuisines of our country.

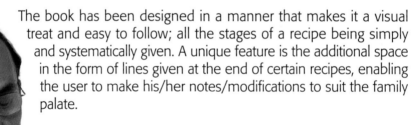

The book has been designed in a manner that makes it a visual treat and easy to follow; all the stages of a recipe being simply and systematically given. A unique feature is the additional space in the form of lines given at the end of certain recipes, enabling the user to make his/her notes/modifications to suit the family palate.

I welcome any suggestions pertaining to or additions to the recipes given.

Happy cooking!

Sitangsu Chakravarty

snacks

snacks snacks

snacks

snacks

know your ingredients

Turmeric (Haldi)

Turmeric is one of the cheapest spices but very colourful and leaves its mark on whatever it is added to. It has digestive, preservative and antiseptic properties. A small amount of turmeric is enough to flavour and colour the dish; too much will only make the food taste bitter.

Onion Seeds (Kalonji)

Small, triangular shaped, hard black seeds that belong to the onion family. Often confused with black cumin, but the two spices have nothing in common and must never be substituted for one another.

Mango Powder (Amchoor)
Portions of unripe mango are dried in the sun and then ground into a fine powder. Lends a piquant, slightly sour tang to savoury dishes.

paneer chops
cottage cheese and potato cutlets

Preparation time	35 minutes
Cooking time	15 minutes
Serves	4–5

Mustard oil	2 tbsp
Onion (chopped)	1 (medium)
Ginger (chopped)	1"
Cottage Cheese (coarsely pounded)	100 gm
Garam masala	1 tsp
Sugar	½ tsp
Salt	1 tsp
Green chilli (chopped)	3
Green coriander (chopped)	1 tbsp
Cashewnuts (broken & coarsely ground)	1 tbsp
Sultanas	2 tsp
Potato (boiled and peeled)	2 (medium)
White bread slices (soaked in water and squeezed dry)	2
Gram flour	½ cup
Cooking soda (Sodium bicarbonate)	A pinch
Turmeric powder	¼ tsp
Bread crumbs	½ cup
Refined oil	To deep fry

Heat 2 tbsp mustard oil in a pan and bring it to smoking point. Fry the chopped onions and ginger till the onions are soft.

Add the coarsely ground cottage cheese, garam masala, sugar, ½ tsp salt, chillies, green coriander, cashewnuts and sultanas. Fry well and keep aside for stuffing.

Mix boiled potato with soaked bread and knead to a smooth dough. Form potato dough into round patties stuffed with cottage cheese filling into a size of 2½" round and about 1½" thick.

Mix gram flour, baking soda, ½ tsp salt and turmeric powder with water to make a thick batter. Dip the cutlets in the batter, and roll them on a layer of bread crumbs. Dust off the excess crumbs. Repeat the process till all the mixture and potato dough is finished.

Heat refined oil in a kadahi. Deep fry the cutlets to golden brown. Drain. Serve as a tea-time snack.

poha (chivda)
pressed rice snack
Maharashtra

Preparation time	10 minutes
Cooking time	15 minutes
Serves	4

Dry pressed rice	1 cup
Refined oil	2 tbsp
Mustard seeds (brown)	1 tsp
Cumin seeds	½ tsp
Asafoetida	1 pinch
Onion (chopped)	1 (medium)
Tomato (chopped)	1 (medium)
Peanuts (unsalted & skinned)	⅓ cup
Turmeric powder	½ tsp
Chilli powder	½ tsp
Ginger (finely chopped)	1 tsp
Salt	To taste (¾ tsp)
Green chilli (finely chopped)	2
Water	4–6 tbsp
Lemon juice	½ lemon
Coconut (grated)	1 tbsp (optional)
Green coriander (chopped)	1 tbsp

Wash the pressed rice in a sieve very carefully under cold running water, drain thoroughly and set aside.

Heat refined oil in a kadahi or wok, add the mustard seeds, cumin seeds and asafoetida. As soon as the seeds start crackling, add chopped onion and fry to a light golden colour and then add chopped tomatoes. Add the peanuts and fry for 3–4 minutes. Next, add turmeric powder, chilli powder, chopped ginger and salt, and stir for a minute or two. Gently add the washed dry pressed rice and chopped green chilli, stir well to mix all the ingredients, sprinkle 5 tbsp water, cover lightly and cook on slow fire for 8–10 minutes until tender.

Now add lemon juice and grated coconut (optional) and mix carefully so as not to break the pressed rice. Sprinkle chopped coriander and serve as a tea-time snack.

dal pakwan

crispy savoury bread with sweet and sour lentil

Maharashtra

Preparation time	15–20 minutes
Cooking time	35–40 minutes
Makes	6–8

Pakwan (thin crispy bread)

Whole wheat flour	2 cups
Plain flour	2 cups
Salt	½ tsp
Ghee/Refined oil	3 tbsp
Red chilli powder	½ tsp
Asafoetida	2 pinches
Water	1½ –2 cups
Refined oil	To fry

For lentil

Bengal gram (cleaned and soaked)	2½ cups
Chilli powder	1½ tsp
Mango powder	2½ tsp
Turmeric powder	1 tsp
Salt	To taste (2 tsp)
Sugar	2 tsp
Ghee	2 tbsp
Green chilli (finely chopped)	4
Garam masala	½ tsp
Tomato sauce	4 tbsp
Water	4–5 cups

Knead the flour, salt, ghee, red chilli powder and asafoetida to a stiff dough by adding water very carefully. The stiffer the dough, the more crisp will be the pakwans. Once the dough is ready, keep it aside for some time.

In the meantime boil the Bengal gram in a saucepan or pressure cooker till soft but the grains should be visible.

Now add chilli powder, mango powder, turmeric powder, salt and sugar. Mix well, bring it to a boil, then let it simmer for 6–8 minutes. Keep aside.

Now make small balls of flour dough to a size of 1½" each. Roll each to 4" to 5" dice. Prick with a fork and deep fry till crisp and brown in colour.

Drain thoroughly and reserve for use, when required. It can be kept in airtight containers for 4–5 days.

Heat 2 tbsp ghee in a pan and fry the green chillies and garam masala. Pour this over the dal. Add tomato sauce to the dal, mix well and serve with pakwan.

upma
savoury semolina with peas and potato
Tamil Nadu

		Preparation time	25–30 minutes
		Cooking time	15–20 minutes
		Serves	6–8

Semolina (preferably the coarse variety)	2 cups	Heat a tawa or frying pan and dry-roast the semolina to golden brown. Keep aside. Boil the green peas and potato cubes, drain and set aside.
Green peas (shelled)	1 cup	
Potato (cut into small cubes)	2 (medium)	
Vegetable oil	4 tbsp	Heat the vegetable oil in a large pan. Add mustard and cumin seeds. When the seeds start crackling, add chopped onion, ginger and curry leaves.
Mustard seed	1 tsp	
Cumin seed	½ tsp	
Onion (chopped)	2 (medium)	
Curry leaves	12–14	
Tomato (chopped)	2 (medium)	When the onions are soft, add chopped tomatoes and green chillies, and fry for 3–4 minutes. Now add the boiled vegetables, salt and sugar and stir well. Add 5 cups of water and bring to a boil.
Green chilli (chopped)	4	
Ginger (chopped)	2 tsp	
Salt	To taste (1 tsp)	Gradually add roasted semolina to the water, stirring continuously. Cook on low fire, till a nearly dry and soft texture is reached. Add the lemon juice and mix well. Keep it covered for 4–5 minutes.
Water	3–4 cups	
Lemon juice	1 lemon	
Coconut (grated)	½ cup	
Green coriander	½ cup	Sprinkle grated coconut and chopped coriander before serving. Upma is generally eaten for breakfast or as a tea-time snack.

amavadai
lentil cutlets
Tamil Nadu

Preparation time	25 minutes+ soaking time
Cooking time	15 minutes
Makes	12–14

Bengal gram (washed and soaked for 3–4 hrs)	2 cups
Coconut (grated)	1 cup
Onion (chopped)	2 (medium)
Green chilli (deseeded and chopped)	3–4
Cooking Soda (Sodium bicarbonate)	1 generous pinch
Chilli powder	1 tsp
Ginger (chopped)	2 tsp
Curry leaves	10–12
Salt	To taste (1½ tsp)
Turmeric powder	½ tsp
Refined oil	To fry, approx. 1½ cup

Drain the excess water from the Bengal gram and grind coarsely. Mix the grated coconut, chopped onion, chopped green chillies, soda bicarbonate, chilli powder, chopped ginger, shredded curry leaves. Mix well. Leave it to rest for 4–5 minutes.

Add salt and turmeric powder and make into soft dough. Make evenly sized 12–14 small balls from the dough. Heat 1½ cup of oil in a non stick frying pan. Flatten the lentil balls by pressing between your palms and fry gently in batches. The cutlets should be crisp and well cooked. Serve as snack for high tea or breakfast with coconut chutney.

dahi kabab
grilled curd (yoghurt) kabab
Madhya Pradesh

Preparation time	20 minutes
Cooking time	45 minutes
Makes	18–20

Chick pea (roasted & powdered)	1 cup
Salt	To taste (2 tsp)
Red chilli powder	2 tsp
Hung curd	1½ cup
Garam masala	1 tsp
Black pepper powder	½ tsp
Ghee	½ cup
Onion (thinly sliced)	1 (medium)
Ginger (chopped)	2 tsp
Garlic (chopped)	3–4 cloves
Milk	3–4 tbsp
Green coriander (chopped)	2 tbsp

Mix roasted chick pea powder, 1 tsp salt and 1 tsp chilli powder with hung curd. Add ½ tsp of garam masala and pepper powder to the curd and mix well.

Now divide this into 20 balls of about 2", gently press between wet palms and give a flat, rounded patty shape. Make sure that the sides are smooth and evenly shaped. Keep aside, covered with a wet cloth.

Heat ghee in a non stick frying pan; when hot enough, slide kababs gently into the frying pan and fry until golden brown. Fry 3–4 at a time. Drain properly, keep on a kitchen paper or towel and keep aside.

Now fry the sliced onion in the same ghee to make them brown and crisp. Remove with a slotted spoon, cool and make a fine paste in a blender or food processor.

Add the remaining 1 tsp chilli powder, chopped ginger, chopped garlic, 1 tsp salt and the ground fried onion in the ghee. Fry well for 5–7 minutes. Next, add ½ tsp garam masala and continue frying for a further 5–7 minutes. Finally, add the fried kababs and mix with the onion masala very gently. Sprinkle milk and mix well, turning the kababs. Serve hot, sprinkled with chopped green coriander.

Serve as a snack or even as part of a vegetarian main meal.

alubukhara-khajur na ghugra
prune and date snack

Gujarat

Preparation time	40 minutes
Cooking time	20–25 minutes
Serves	4–6

Coconut (grated)	½ cup
Sesame seeds	2 tsp
Apricot (dried & roughly ground)	¾ cup
Dates (seedless & roughly ground)	¾ cup
Green cardamom (powdered)	¼ tsp
Sugar (powdered)	½ cup
Milk	½ cup
Salt	½ tsp
Plain flour	1 cup
Ghee	½ cup
Refined oil	To deep fry

Make a smooth mixture of coconut, sesame seeds, apricots, dates, cardamom powder and sugar in a blender by adding a little milk (approximately ¼ cup).

Make even-sized balls (about 10–12) of the mixture.

Mix salt with the flour and rub ½ cup ghee thoroughly. Add ¼ cup milk and prepare a dough. Knead the dough for at least 10 minutes to smoothen it properly.

Make 10–12 equal portions and shape into balls. Roll out each ball of flour into 3–4" circles. Fill the date and apricot mixture. Fold into half to look like semi-circles. Seal the edges by tightly pressing with the fingertips.

Heat the refined oil in a kadahi, deep frying the balls in batches on medium heat till golden brown.

Drain and keep aside. Serve as a sweet snack.

paneer tikkas
grilled cottage cheese
Delhi

Preparation time	15 minutes + marinating time
Cooking time	12–15 minutes
Serves	4

Cottage cheese	500 gm
Hung curd	1 cup
Ginger paste	2 tsp
Garlic paste	2 tsp
Mustard oil	2 tbsp
Chilli powder	1 tsp
Turmeric powder	1 tsp
Salt	To taste
White pepper powder	1 tsp
Lemon juice	1 lemon
Garam masala	½ tsp
Onion (sliced)	1
Lemon (cut to wedges)	1

Cut the paneer into 1″ thick slices and then into 2″ squares.

Mix the curd and ginger–garlic paste in a big bowl. Add mustard oil, chilli powder, turmeric powder, salt, pepper, lemon juice and the garam masala powder, and mix thoroughly.

Now add the paneer cubes and rub the marinade very gently into each paneer cube. Leave to marinate for an hour.

Skewer the paneer pieces and bake in a pre-heated oven (400°F) or grill over charcoal or under a very hot grill for about 4–5 minutes until the paneer turns brown.

Serve sprinkled with chaat masala and with raw, sliced onion and lemon wedges.

pakora
batter fried vegetables
Allover India

Preparation time	25 minutes
Cooking time	15 minutes
Serves	4

Potato	1 (medium)
Aubergine	1 (medium)
Onion	2 (medium)
Green chilli	4–8
Gram flour	2 cups
Chilli powder	1 tsp
Cumin seeds	1/2 tsp
Salt	To taste (1 tsp)
Cooking soda (sodium bicarbonate)	1/2 tsp
Water	1 cup
Refined oil	To deep fry

Peel and cut the potato into 1/4" thick round slices. Cut the aubergine in slices of the same thickness. Peel and slice the onion in 1/4" roundels. Deseed the green chillies. Set the vegetables aside.

Combine gram flour, chilli powder, cumin seeds, salt and soda bicarbonate and mix well. Add approx 3/4 to 1 cup of water to make a very thick batter of coating consistency. Heat the refined oil in a kadahi. Make sure the oil is hot enough otherwise the pakoras will absorb oil and become soggy.

Dip the vegetables, one at a time into the batter, coating them thoroughly. Deep fry for 2–3 minutes till half cooked, then remove and keep aside.

Just before serving the pakoras, reheat the oil and fry the pakoras until golden brown and crisp. Serve hot as tea-time snacks with tomato sauce or mint chutney.

adai cutlets
vegetable in rice-lentil pancake

Tamil Nadu

Preparation time	25 minutes + soaking time
Cooking time	20–25 minutes
Makes	15–20

Rice	½ cup
Bengal gram	½ cup
Black gram	½ cup
Split yellow lentil	½ cup
Asafoetida	¼ tsp
Salt	1½ tsp
Green chilli	4–5
Ginger	1"
Garlic	4 cloves
Coconut (grated)	1 tbsp
Turmeric powder	½ tsp
Coriander powder	1 tsp
Cumin powder	1 tsp
Refined oil	3 tbsp
Mustard seeds	½ tsp
Onion (chopped)	1 (big)
Beetroot (shredded)	1 (small)
Carrot	1 (medium)
Potato (thinly sliced)	1 (medium)
Cabbage (shredded)	½ (small)
Green peas (shelled)	½ cup
French beans (thin slices)	½ cup
Green coriander (chopped)	2 tbsp

Soak the rice and lentils for 6–8 cutlets. Drain and grind to a paste with asafoetida and ¾ tsp salt, adding water to form a thick batter.

Grind together green chillies, ginger, garlic, grated coconut, turmeric powder, coriander and cumin powder to a fine paste with 2 tbsp water.

Heat the refined oil in a saucepan and add the mustard seeds. When they start popping add all the vegetables and fry for 3–4 minutes. Now add the ground paste, ¾ tsp salt and green coriander, cover and cook till the vegetables are done. Set aside.

Heat a griddle. Smear it well with oil. Put 2 tbsp batter (rice and dal) and spread it to a thin round about 4" in diameter.

Spread 1 to 1½ tbsp cooked vegetables evenly on the surface of the pancake. Pour another 2 tbsp batter on top and cover the vegetables carefully.

Cover and cook over moderate heat for 2 minutes. Turn over and fry both sides to a golden colour.

Serve hot as a snack with chutney.

kalakals
crispy biscuits
Goa

Preparation time	20 minutes
Cooking time	15–20 minutes
Makes	10–12

Plain refined flour	2 cups
Cooking Soda (Sodium bicarbonate)	A generous pinch
Nutmeg (grated)	½ tsp
Salt	To taste (½ tsp)
Ghee	2 tbsp
Egg (beaten)	1
Sugar	1 tbsp
Coconut milk	½ cup
Refined oil	For deep frying

Sieve the flour with soda bicarbonate, nutmeg and salt. Rub the ghee in the flour to mix well. Add the beaten egg, sugar and coconut milk, and make a dough. Knead for 5–6 minutes to make it smooth.

Now divide the dough into 10–12 equal sized balls. Set aside covered with a damp cloth for 15–20 minutes. Press and make each ball into an oval shape like a shell of about 2". Make any design with a toothpick or fork.

Put a kadahi or wok on fire and heat enough refined oil to fry the fritters. Deep fry kalakals a few at a time on moderate heat till brown and crisp.

Cool and store in airtight containers. Serve as tea-time snacks.

kachauri
peas-stuffed fried bread
West Bengal

Preparation time	35–40 minutes
Cooking time	15 minutes
Makes	14–16

Filling

Green peas (shelled)	2–3 cups
Ghee	1 tbsp
Asafoetida	2 pinches
Onion seeds	½ tsp
Aniseed	½ tsp
Chilli powder	½ tsp
Black pepper powder	½ tsp
Salt	½ tsp
Sugar	½ tsp

Dough

Plain flour	4 cup
Soda bicarbonate	A pinch
Vegetable oil/Ghee	2 tbsp
Salt	To taste (½ tsp)
Refined oil	To deep fry

Grind the peas to form a paste.

Heat 1 tbsp ghee in a pan. Add asafoetida and onion seeds. When the seeds start crackling, add the pea paste and other spices like aniseed, chilli powder, pepper powder, salt and sugar. Stir-fry for 3–4 minutes till the masalas are well mixed with peas. Keep aside.

Sieve the flour with salt and soda bicarbonate. Rub 2 tbsp ghee in the flour till it becomes crumbly. Add enough water (approximately 1 cup) to make dough. Knead for 10–12 minutes till the dough is soft and pliable.

Now divide the dough into 14–16 even roundels and keep covered with a wet cloth. Stuff each roundel of dough with 1 tsp filling by making a depression with the thumb. Seal carefully and roll on a floured surface to 4" round and 1/8" thick.

Heat the refined oil in a kadahi. Deep fry the kachauri one at a time, turning over each side to get an even, golden colour. Remove from oil with a perforated spoon, draining thoroughly the excess oil.

Serve as per requirement.

vegetables

know your ingredients

Asafoetida (Hing)

Asafoetida can be bought in solid form or as a powder. It has an extremely interesting flavour and aroma when used in minute quantities in cooking, but gives a very pungent smell on account of the sulphur compounds in it. It counteracts flatulence and is always added to pulses, beans and green vegetables.

Mustard Seeds (Rai or Sarson)

Mustard belongs to the spinach family and is used as a green vegetable in north India. There are three varieties of mustard seeds — black, brown or Indian mustard, and white (alba) mustard. To obtain the full flavour of the seeds, they must be fried quickly in very hot oil.

Coriander (Dhaniya)

The seeds are used as a spice and the fresh leaves as a herb. The small seeds are more aromatic when dry roasted lightly and then ground into a fine powder.

sabzi miloni
mixed vegetables

Preparation time	40–45 minutes
Cooking time	20–25 minutes
Serves	6–8

Mustard oil	4 tbsp
Paanch foran (see page 160)	1 tsp
Onion (chopped)	2 (medium)
Bay leaf	2
Green chilli	4
Ginger paste	1 tbsp
Cauliflower (cut into 1½" florets)	1 (approx. 300–400gm)
Cabbage (cut into 1" dice)	1 (approx. 300–400gm)
Carrot (1" dice)	3–4 (medium)
Beans (cut into 1" pieces)	1 cup
Green peas (shelled)	1 cup
Cumin powder	2 tsp
Coriander powder	1 tbsp
Turmeric powder	1 tsp
Chilli powder	1 tsp
Water	2 cups (approx.)
Salt	To taste (1½ tsp)
Garam masala	½ tsp

Heat mustard oil in a saucepan. When the oil reaches smoking point, put the paanch foran in the oil. It starts crackling immediately.

Add the onions and fry for 3–4 minutes till they become soft. Next add the bay leaves and green chilli, slit length-wise. Put in the ginger paste and fry for 2–3 minutes.

Now add all the vegetables and fry for 4–5 minutes. Add all the spices except garam masala. Fry till the spices are well browned and give a pleasing aroma. If it sticks on the pan, add a tablespoon of water from time to time.

Fry the vegetables for 8–10 minutes on a slow fire. Add enough water to cover the vegetables. Mix salt and cover and cook for 7–8 minutes till the vegetables are tender and the gravy has thickened.

Sprinkle garam masala powder and serve hot with puries or parathas.

konkani aloo matar
potato green pea curry
Goa

Preparation time		10–15 minutes
Cooking time		15–20 minutes
Serves		4–6

Dry coconut	½	
Dried red chilli	3–4	
Green chilli	4	
Ginger	2"	
Garlic	4 cloves	
Poppy seeds	2 tsp	
Cashewnut	20	
Refined oil	4–5 tbsp	
Turmeric powder	1 tsp	
Cumin powder	2 tsp	
Coriander powder	2 tsp	
Salt	To taste (1½ tsp)	
Potato (peeled and cut into 1x8 dice)	4 (medium)	
Green peas (shelled)	1 cup	
Tamarind pulp	1 tbsp	
Water	2 cups	
Green coriander (chopped)	2 tbsp	

Grind coconut, chillies, ginger, garlic, poppy seeds and half of the cashewnuts (adding 3–4 tbsp of water) to a paste.

Heat the vegetable oil in a heavy base saucepan. Fry the paste till the mixture leaves the oil.

Add all the spices and salt. Next add potatoes, peas and the remaining cashewnuts, and fry for 3–4 minutes on a low fire.

Now add the tamarind pulp and 2 cups of water. Cover and cook till the vegetables are done. Transfer to a serving dish and sprinkle chopped green coriander. Serve with plain boiled rice.

avial
mixed vegetable with coconut
Tamil Nadu

Preparation time	30 minutes
Cooking time	30 minutes
Serves	4–6

Water	
Salt	To taste (1½ tsp)
Turmeric powder	1 tsp
Carrot	2
(peeled and ½" diced)	
Potato (peeled &	2 (medium)
¾" diced)	
Cashewnuts	10–12
Green peas (shelled)	1 cup
Beans (½"cut)	1 cup
Raw bananas	2
(peeled and ½" diced)	
Cabbage (shredded)	1 cup
Curd	1 cup
Refined oil	2 tbsp
(traditionally	
coconut oil)	
Fenugreek seeds	½ tsp
Cumin seeds	½ tsp
Curry leaves	10–12

For ground spice paste

Coconut (grated)	1
Cumin seeds	2 tsp
Black peppercorn	½ tsp
Mustard seeds (brown)	1 tsp
Green chilli	8–10
Rice (washed)	1½ tsp

Bring 3–4 cups of water to a boil in a saucepan. Add the salt and turmeric to water. Next, add carrots and potatoes and boil them for 3–4 minutes. Then, add cashewnuts, peas, beans and raw banana and boil for another 3 minutes.

Now add the cabbage and boil for 2 minutes. Drain and reserve the water to be used later.

Put the saucepan on the fire with the boiled vegetables in it. Mix curd (well beaten) and ground spice paste to the vegetables. Stir for a while, add enough reserved water to make a thick consistency for the gravy.

Heat 2 tbsp oil in a small pan, add the fenugreek seeds, cumin seeds and curry leaves. When they start popping, pour over the vegetable curry and mix very gently. Cover and leave to rest for 2 minutes. It is served hot with puris or steamed rice.

saag bhaja
pan fried spinach
West Bengal

Preparation time	10 minutes
Cooking time	25 minutes
Serves	4

Fresh spinach (thoroughly washed and dried)	1kg
Mustard oil	3 tbsp
Paanch foran (see Page 160)	1 tsp
Green chilli	2
Salt	To taste (½ tsp)
Turmeric powder	½ tsp

Wash the spinach leaves thoroughly in water. Drain and remove the stalks.

Heat oil in a large saucepan as initially the spinach will need space for its leafy texture. When the oil reaches smoking point add the paanch foran and green chilli.

When the seeds and chilli start crackling, lower the heat and add the spinach, salt and turmeric powder. Cover and cook for 8–10 minutes till the spinach is tender.

Remove the lid and cook the spinach till it is nearly dry. If there is a lot of water (generally spinach leaves a lot of water on cooking) increase the heat and dry the moisture faster. Serve hot. This is generally the first course of a meal in West Bengal.

aloo dum
potatoes in spicy sauce
West Bengal

Preparation time	10 minutes
Cooking time	25 minutes
Serves	4

Ginger (fresh)	1"
Cumin seeds	1 tsp
Tomato	2 (medium)
Turmeric powder	½ tsp
Coriander powder	1½ tsp
Chilli powder	1 tsp
Mustard oil	4 tbsp
Bay leaf	2
Asafoetida	2 pinches
Baby potato	500 gm
(If not available, regular medium sized potato can be used, cut into 4)	
Water	1½ cup
Salt	To taste (1tsp)
Curd	3 tbsp
Ghee	1 tbsp
Garam masala	1 tsp

Put ginger, cumin seeds and one tomato in a blender to make a smooth paste. Add turmeric, chilli and coriander powder to the paste and blend for 1–2 minutes. Keep the paste aside.

Heat the oil to smoking point. Add the bay leaves and asafoetida. Next, add the potatoes and fry on a slow fire till they are golden brown.

Now add the ginger and spice paste and stir thoroughly for 5–7 minutes. To this add the balance tomatoes, roughly chopped. Cover and cook for 10 minutes. If necessary, add 1 tbsp water.

Add salt and half the water, cover with a lid, and cook until the potatoes are tender. In the meantime stir the curd in a bowl to a smooth consistency.

Remove the lid, add the remaining water, bring it to a boil and mix thoroughly. When the sauce is reduced, oil separates in the pan.

Heat the ghee in a round spoon. Add the garam masala powder and fry for 1–2 minutes. Sprinkle the ghee on the potato and cover with a lid immediately.

Remove from fire and transfer to a serving dish. Serve with puri or chapattis.

bhaja mung dal
roasted yellow lentil

West Bengal

Preparation time	15 minutes
Cooking time	40 minutes
Serves	6–8

Yellow lentil	1 cup
Water	2½ cup
Bay leaf	4
Green chilli (slit)	2
Salt	To taste (2 tsp)
Sugar	½ tsp
Ghee	1 tbsp
Cumin seeds	1 tsp
Red chilli (whole, dry)	4 (medium)
Fresh ginger (thin strips)	1"
Turmeric powder	1 tsp

Heat a thick bottomed saucepan or pressure cooker and dry-roast the yellow lentil till it is golden brown in colour and gives a roast aroma.

Wash the lentil and boil it, adding the water, bay leaves and green chilli. Pressure cook it for 5–7 minutes. Add salt and sugar and simmer for another 10 minutes till the lentil is cooked.

In a saucepan heat 1 tbsp ghee. Add cumin seeds, dry red chilli, ginger julienne and turmeric powder. Fry for a few minutes. Pour the cooked lentil in it and simmer for five minutes covering the pan. Adjust seasoning and serve hot with boiled rice.

paneer hare pyaaz wala
cottage cheese with spring onion
Delhi

Preparation time	15 minutes
Cooking time	25–30 minutes
Serves	4

Refined oil	4 tbsp
Cumin seeds	½ tsp
Ginger (thin julienne)	1"
Onion (sliced)	1 (medium)
Turmeric powder	½ tsp
Chilli powder	½ tsp
Black pepper powder	¼ tsp
Salt	To taste (1 tsp)
Spring onion (white, sliced)	1 cup
Tomato (sliced)	1 (medium)
Green coriander (chopped)	2 tbsp
Cottage cheese (cut into 1½" fingers)	500 gm
Green chilli (slit lengthwise)	3

Heat refined oil in a wide pan. Add cumin seeds and ginger julienne. When the seeds start crackling, add sliced onion and fry till they are soft.

Now add turmeric powder, chilli powder and black pepper powder, and stir for a while. Add salt and spring onions and mix thoroughly. Put in the tomatoes, and green chillies. Cover and cook for 2–3 minutes on a low fire.

Now add the cottage cheese fingers and mix very gently. See that the edges of the cubes do not break and the onion tomato mixture is well blended with the cottage cheese. Cover and cook for 5–6 minutes.

Transfer to a serving dish. Sprinkle chopped green coriander on top. Serve with chapattis and raita.

vegetable kootu
mixed vegetables
Kerala

Preparation time	15 minutes
Cooking time	20–25 minutes
Serves	4

Refined oil	2 tbsp
Mustard seeds (brown)	1 tsp
Curry leaves	8–10
Onion (chopped)	2 (medium)
Tomato (chopped)	1 (medium)
Turmeric powder	1½ tsp
Chilli powder	1 tsp
Coriander powder	1½ tsp
Cumin powder	1 tsp
Potato (diced ½")	2 (medium)
French beans (chopped ½")	¾ cup
Red pumpkin (diced ½")	1 cup
Carrot (diced ½")	1 large
Broad beans (chopped ½")	¾ cup
Drumstick (cut into 1½")	2
Salt	To taste
Black pepper (crushed)	6–8
Water	1 cup
Coconut milk	½ cup
Green chilli	3–4

Heat the refined oil in a heavy base saucepan. When the oil is hot, put in the mustard seeds and curry leaves. The seeds starts popping. Now add chopped onion and fry for 2–3 minutes.

Then add chopped tomato, turmeric powder, chilli powder, coriander powder and cumin powder. Fry for another 3–4 minutes. Now add all the vegetables.

Put in salt, crushed black pepper and 1 cup of water, cover and cook on a low fire for 10–12 minues or until the vegetables are nearly done.

Finally, add coconut milk and slit green chillies, let this simmer for 5 minutes till the vegetables are tender and the sauce has thickened. Serve hot with puris or rice.

cheese pakora kalia
cheese fritters in gravy
Uttar Pradesh

Preparation time	20–25 minutes
Cooking time	30–35 minutes
Serves	4–6

For Pakora

Plain flour	1 cup
Processed cheese (grated)	¾ cup
Onion (finely chopped)	1 (medium)
Baking powder	½ tsp
Ginger powder	½ tsp
Yellow mustard seeds (powder)	½ tsp
Red chilli powder	½ tsp
Green chilli (finely chopped)	2 tsp
Salt	To taste
Water	½ -¾ cup
Vegetable oil	To deep fry

For Kalia (curry)

Onion	1 (big) 2 (medium)
Ginger	1" dice
Garlic	3 cloves
Refined oil	4 tbsp
Cumin powder	1 tsp
Coriander powder	1 tsp
Garam masala	½ tsp
Tomato	3 (medium)
Salt	To taste (1 tsp)
Water	2 cups
Cashewnuts (fried)	10–12
Green coriander (chopped)	2 tbsp

Mix together all the ingredients for pakora with enough water to form a thick batter. Set aside for 10 minutes.

Heat enough vegetable oil in a saucepan or kadahi to smoking point, reduce heat and with a teaspoon drop the batter into the hot oil.

Fry six to eight pakoras at a time to a golden brown colour. Drain and keep aside.

To make kalia or curry, grind onion, ginger and garlic to a fine paste. Heat 4 tbsp oil in a heavy base saucepan. Add the onion paste and fry till it is light brown in colour and the onions are cooked. Add the spices and stir-fry for another 2 minutes.

Add the tomatoes with juices and cook till they are of soft consistency.

Add salt and water and boil for a few minutes. Add the pakoras and simmer for 2–3 minutes. Transfer into a serving dish. Sprinkle fried cashew nuts and green coriander before serving.

methi pakori curry
fenugreek kofta curry
Delhi

Preparation time	15 minutes
Cooking time	30 minutes
Serves	4–6

Pakori

Fresh fenugreek (cleaned and chopped)	250 gm
Gram flour	1 cup
Plain flour	¼ cup
Chilli powder	½ tsp
Coriander powder	1 tsp
Cumin powder	½ tsp
Salt	To taste (½ tsp)
Water	½ cup
Refined oil	To fry

Curry masala

Vegetable oil	3 tbsp
Cumin seeds	1 tsp
Onion (chopped)	2 (medium)
Ginger paste	1 tsp
Garlic paste	1 tsp
Tomato (chopped)	2 (medium)
Water	2 cups
Chilli powder	½ tsp
Turmeric powder	1 tsp
Salt	To taste (1 tsp)
Green coriander	1 tbsp

Heat 3 tbsp oil in a saucepan and add the cumin seeds. When they start crackling, add the chopped onion and fry for 2–3 minutes. Now add the ginger and garlic paste and fry till the mixture is golden brown.

Next, add the chopped tomatoes and fry them till they are pulpy in texture. If the mixture sticks to the bottom, add one or two tablespoons of water.

Add the chilli powder, turmeric and salt. Stir for a little while, then add the remaining water and bring it to a boil. Simmer for 10–12 minutes and set aside.

To make the pakori, mix fenugreek leaves together with gram flour, flour, and all the spices plus salt in a bowl. Adding water slowly, form a thick paste.

Heat oil in a kadai for frying. Now take about 1½ tsp fenugreek mixture, shape into a ball and drop it into the hot oil. Fry to a deep golden colour, a few at a time.

Put the fried pakoris in the sauce and simmer for 10 minutes.

Sprinkle with chopped coriander leaves. Serve with steamed or boiled rice.

bhindi do pyaza
okra with onion
Punjab

Preparation time	15 minutes
Cooking time	15 minutes
Serves	4

Okra	500 gm
Vegetable oil	2 tbsp
Cumin seeds	½ tsp
Onion (thinly sliced)	3 (medium)
Bay leaf	1
Green chilli (slit)	1
Chilli powder	½ tsp
Turmeric powder	½ tsp
Tomato (cut into half and sliced)	2 (medium)
Salt	To taste (1 tsp)
Green coriander (chopped)	1 tbsp

Wash and pat dry the okra. Remove the heads and cut into 1" size. Keep aside. Do not wash after cutting.

Heat oil in a pan, then add the cumin seeds. When they splutter, add the sliced onion, bay leaf and green chilli, stirring continiously. Fry the onion into a golden brown colour.

Now add the chilli powder, turmeric powder, tomatoes and salt. Fry for 2 minutes, then add the okra. Mix well and cover the pan. Cook for approximately 10 minutes on a slow fire, stirring periodically. Cook till the okra is tender and retains its shape and colour.

Transfer to a serving dish. Sprinkle chopped coriander and serve with paratha and lentil. It is also a good accompaniment to a chicken dish.

rajma masala
red kidney beans
Delhi

Preparation time 15 minutes+
8–10 hrs for soaking
Cooking time 50–55 minutes, less in
pressure cooker
Serves 4–6

Red kidney beans (soaked overnight)	1 cup
Water	4 cups
Refined oil	2 tbsp
Bay leaf	2
Cumin seeds	1 tsp
Onion (finely chopped)	2 (medium)
Garlic (chopped)	1 clove
Ginger (finely chopped)	1 tsp
Chilli powder	1 tsp
Turmeric powder	½ tsp
Coriander powder	1½ tsp
Tomato (chopped)	2 (medium)
Green chilli (chopped)	1
Salt	To taste (1½ tsp)
Green coriander (chopped)	2 tbsp

Wash the soaked red kidney beans and place them in a saucepan with enough water. Put the bay leaves and cook till the skin is cracked and bean is tender. It can be cooked in a pressure cooker for approximately 20 minutes.

To prepare the masala, heat oil in a pan, then add the cumin seeds. They start crackling immediately.

Now add the onion, ginger and garlic. Fry until the onion is soft and golden brown in colour.

Add the chilli powder, turmeric powder and coriander powder. Fry for 4–5 minutes till the spices blend well.

Add the tomatoes and green chilli and stir well. Fry for 7–8 minutes till the onion-tomato mixture becomes pulpy and the oil separates from it.

Next add the cooked beans to it. Stir well and simmer on a slow fire, covering the pan. Add salt and mix thoroughly. Cook for a few more minutes, mashing a few beans with the back of the ladle to give a good consistency.

Check the seasoning before removing from the fire. Sprinkle chopped green coriander and serve hot with boiled rice.

matar paneer
peas and cheese curry
Punjab

Preparation time	15 minutes
Cooking time	30 minutes
Serves	4

Onion	2 (medium)
Ginger	1½ "
Garlic	2 cloves
Green chilli	1
Vegetable oil	2 tbsp
Fenugreek seeds	½ tsp
Onion seeds	½ tsp
Cumin seeds	1 tsp
Water	1½ cup
Turmeric powder	½ tsp
Coriander powder	2 tsp
Chilli powder	1 tsp
Salt	To taste (2 tsp)
Tomatoes (chopped)	2 (medium)
Green peas (shelled)	250 gm
Cottage cheese	300gm
(cut into 1"x ½" cubes)	
Garam masala	½ tsp
Coriander (chopped)	2 tbsp

In a blender grind together onion, ginger, garlic and green chilli to a smooth paste.

Heat oil in a saucepan, add the fenugreek seeds, onion seeds and cumin seeds. As soon as they crackle, add the onion paste and fry till golden brown.

Add a few tablespoons of water if necessary to prevent the paste sticking to the bottom.

Add turmeric, coriander, chilli powder and salt. Fry for 5–6 minutes, add the chopped tomatoes and stir well. Cook till the tomatoes are mashed and separate from the oil. Add the green peas. Fry for another few minutes, add the remaining water and cover with a lid.

Cook on a slow fire for 10 minutes or until the peas are tender. Gently drop the cottage cheese cubes into the mixture and cook for another 5 minutes till they are very tender and the sauce is thick.

Add the garam masala and chopped green coriander. Cover and simmer for 4–5 minutes. Transfer to a serving dish and serve hot. Serve with chapatties/parathas along with lentil.

mungeri aloo
fried potato dumplings in spicy onion sauce
Bihar

Preparation time	30 minutes
Cooking time	35 minutes
Serves	4–6

Potato	6–8 (medium)
Salt	To taste
Ginger (finely chopped)	1"
Green coriander (chopped)	2 tbsp
Green chilli (finely chopped)	3
Peanuts (roasted and roughly chopped)	3 tbsp
Flour	3 tbsp
Vegetable oil	½ cup
Onion (thinly sliced)	4 (medium)
Turmeric powder	1 tsp
Coriander powder	1½ tsp
Chilli powder	¾ tsp
Ginger powder	½ tsp
Tomato	2 (medium)
Water	2 cups
Garam masala	½ tsp

Boil potatoes till tender. Remove from water and cool. Now peel and mash them. Add ¾ tsp salt and mix well. Add chopped ginger, coriander, green chilli in the potato mixture and make a smooth dough.

Take one tablespoon of the mixture at a time in your palm, stuff small broken peanuts and shape into a smooth ball. Repeat the process, using all the potato mixture. Dust with flour and cool it in a refrigerator.

Now heat oil in a deep pan or kadahi and fry the potato balls to a golden brown colour. Strain and keep aside.

Heat 2 tbsp oil in a saucepan and fry the sliced onion till it turns golden brown. Now add the turmeric, chilli, coriander and ginger powder and fry for a few minutes. Add the chopped tomatoes and stir to blend well. Add a little water and cook till the oil separates.

Add the remaining water and salt and cook for 8–10 minutes. Now lower the heat and simmer until the sauce thickens.

Drop the potato balls in the sauce and sprinkle garam masala and some green coriander.

Remove from fire, and leave it in the same saucepan, covered, for 7–8 minutes. Serve with paratha or chapattis.

kabuli chana
white chick peas

Preparation time	15 minutes+ soaking time (10 hrs)
Cooking time	30–35 minutes, less in pressure cooker
Serves	4

White chick peas (soaked overnight)	1 cup
Cooking soda (sodium bicarborate)	½ tsp
Water	4 cups
Vegetable oil	3 tbsp
Bay leaves	2
Cumin seeds	1 tsp
Onion (chopped)	3 (medium)
Ginger (chopped)	1 tsp
Garlic (finely chopped)	3 cloves
Green chilli (chopped)	2
Turmeric powder	1 tsp
Red chilli powder	1 tsp
Coriander powder	2 tsp
Tomato (chopped)	2 (medium)
Salt	To taste (1½ tsp)
Lemon juice	1 lemon
Green coriander (chopped)	1 tbsp
Garam masala	1 tsp

Boil the chick peas with cooking soda till they are tender. If cooked in a pressure cooker, reduce the water by ¾ quantity. When the chick peas are boiled leave them in the same water to rest.

Heat oil in a large saucepan or frying pan. Add the bay leaves and cumin seeds. As soon as they crackle, add the chopped onion, ginger, garlic and green chilli, stir well and fry till the onions are golden brown.

Add the turmeric powder, chilli powder and coriander powder. Stir well and add the tomatoes. Mix well and fry for 7–8 minutes or till the tomatoes are mashed thoroughly and oil starts separating from the mixture.

Pour the onion and tomato mixture into the boiled chick peas and stir thoroughly. Add salt and lemon juice and bring it to a boil. Reduce heat and let it simmer for 10–12 minutes, covering the vessel. Sprinkle chopped green coriander and garam masala. Serve hot with jeera pulao (page 128)

lobhiya tamatarwala
black-eyed beans with tomatoes
Delhi

Preparation time	15–20 minutes+ soaking time
Cooking time	1 hr
Serves	4–6

Vegetable oil	4 tbsp
Cinnamon	2" stick
Green cardamom	4
Bay leaf	2
Onion (chopped)	3 (medium)
Ginger (chopped)	1 tbsp
Garlic (chopped)	2 cloves
Tomato (chopped)	3 (medium)
Turmeric powder	1 tsp
Coriander powder	1 tbsp
Cumin powder	2 tsp
Chilli powder	1 tsp
Salt	To taste (2 tsp)
Curd	2 tbsp
Black-eyed bean (soaked overnight)	1 cup
Water	4 cups
Green coriander (chopped)	2 tbsp

Heat the oil in a heavy base saucepan. Add the cinnamon, cardamom and bay leaves and fry for a few minutes.

Now add the chopped onion, ginger and garlic, and fry till the mixture is golden brown in colour. Add a few tablespoons of water if the onions stick to the bottom of the pan. Add the chopped tomatoes and fry for 6–8 minutes until the oil separates.

Now add turmeric powder, coriander powder, cumin powder, chilli powder and salt. Continue frying for another 3–5 minutes. Next, add the curd and stir well. Cook till the oil separates.

Add the drained black-eyed beans and water, and mix well. Bring to a boil, reduce heat, cover and cook for 45 minutes or pressure cook for 15 minutes until the beans are cooked and soft. If required, more water can be added.

Transfer to a serving dish, sprinkle with chopped coriander leaves and serve hot with parathas or chapattis.

arhar ki dal
lentil with vegetable

Preparation time	10–15 minutes
Cooking time	35–40 minutes
Makes	4–6

Yellow lentil	1 cup
Water	6–7 cups
Drumstick (optional) (cut into 1" pieces)	1
Potato (1" cubes)	1 (medium)
White radish (cut into 1" long fingers)	½ cup
Cauliflower (cut into 1" florets)	½ cup
Broad beans (1" diced)	½ cup
Turmeric powder	1 tsp
Chilli powder	1 tsp
Coriander powder	1 tbsp
Cumin powder	1 tbsp
Ginger (chopped)	2 tsp
Green chilli (chopped)	2
Salt	To taste (2 tsp)
Jaggery	1 tbsp
Ghee	2 tbsp
Cumin seeds	1 tsp
Asafoetida	¼ tsp

Wash lentil and put in boiling water in a deep pan or pressure cooker. Stir and let it boil. When the lentil comes to a boil, add the vegetables in a sequence of different stages as per their cooking time, keeping in mind that the lentil will take approximately 25–30 minutes to cook.

Add the turmeric, chilli, coriander, cumin powder, ginger, green chillies, salt and jagggery. Mix thoroughly and simmer for another 5–7 minutes or till the lentil and the vegetables are cooked.

In a separate pan heat ghee, and add the cumin seeds and asafoetida. When it stops spluttering, pour into the lentil, cover and give a boil.

Remove from fire and transfer to a serving dish. Serve hot with parathas or chapattis.

saag masoor dal
red lentil in spinach

West Bengal

Preparation time	10 minutes
Cooking time	25–30 minutes
Serves	4–6

Red lentil	1¼ cup
Spinach (washed and roughly chopped)	1 bunch
Onion (thinly sliced)	1 (medium)
Bay leaf	1
Salt	1 tsp
Water	2 cups
Vegetable oil	1 tbsp
Brown mustard seeds	½ tsp
Cumin seeds	1 tsp
Red chilli (whole, dry)	2
Fresh Ginger (chopped)	½ tsp
Garlic (finely chopped)	1 clove
Asafoetida	¼ tsp
Turmeric powder	½ tsp

Place the lentil, spinach, sliced onion, bay leaf, salt and water in a thick bottomed pan or in a pressure cooker. Boil/pressure cook till the lentil is cooked, and simmer for 7–8 minutes until it thickens to soup consistency.

Heat the vegetable oil in a pan. Add the cumin and mustard seeds and red chilli. When the seeds starts popping, add chopped ginger, garlic, asafoetida, and turmeric powder. Stir for 2 minutes.

Pour the mixture in the lentil and cover. Cook on a slow fire for a few more minutes. Check the seasoning and serve hot. Serve with boiled rice.

chorchori
mixed vegetable

Preparation time	25 minutes
Cooking time	30 minutes
Serves	6–8

Mustard oil	3 tbsp
Paanch foran (see page 160)	½ tsp.
Green chilli (slit lengthwise)	2
Potato (cut into ¼)	3 (medium)
Fresh spinach (cut into 2" pieces)	1 bunch
Salt	To taste (1½ tsp)
Red pumpkin (cut into1½" cube)	300 gm (10–12pieces)
Raddish (cut lengthwise into ½")	1 (medium)
Brinjal (cut into 1½" dice)	1 (medium)
Cauliflower (cut into florets of 1") (the stems can also be added cut into 1")	1 (medium)
Chilli powder	1 tsp
Turmeric powder	1 tsp
Coriander powder	1 tbsp
Sugar (optional)	1 tsp

Heat mustard oil in a deep pan. Allow the oil to come to smoking point. Add paanch foran and the green chilli. When spices start crackling, add the potatoes. Fry for 3–4 minutes, then add the spinach and salt. Cover with a lid. Cook for 10–12 minutes till the spinach is reduced to half.

Add all the vegetables, spices and sugar. Stir thoroughly, cover and cook for another 8–10 minutes, then remove the lid and stir until the water is evaporated. Care should be taken while stirring the chorchori so that the vegetables are not mashed. Its consistency should be nearly dry.

The best way to enjoy chorchori is with boiled/steamed plain rice.

baigan bhurta
spicy roasted brinjals
Delhi

Round brinjal	2 (large)
Vegetable oil	3 tbsp
Onion (finely chopped)	3 (large)
Ginger (finely chopped)	1"
Chilli powder	½ tsp
Tomato (chopped)	3 (large)
Green chilli (chopped)	1
Salt	To taste (1½ tsp)
Garam masala	½ tsp
Green coriander (chopped)	1 tbsp
Ginger (thin julienne)	1"

Preparation time	15 minutes
Cooking time	20 minutes
Serves	4

Wash and dry the brinjal. Rub them with a little oil so that the skin becomes smooth. Give a deep cut in the brinjal lengthwise with a sharp knife. Make sure that the stem is not cut and holds the brinjal.

Spike each brinjal with a fork or skewer and hold it over direct flame of the gas burner. Turning the brinjal a few times, make sure that the skin is completely charred. Remove and cool.

Hold the brinjal by the stalk and remove all the charred skin. Cut off the stalk and discard it. Chop the flesh finely with a sharp knife.

Heat oil in a pan, add the onions, fry for 8–10 minutes till the onions are golden in colour.

Add the chopped ginger, chilli powder, tomatoes and green chilli, fry for 5 minutes and when the tomatoes are totally mashed add the chopped brinjal.

Mix well, add salt and fry the mixture for 10 minutes until it blends well. Do not cover the pan while cooking. Add the garam masala and chopped green coriander and fry for 1–2 minutes.

Remove from heat, garnish with thin julienne of fresh ginger and chopped coriander. Serve hot with lentil and chapattis.

khatti arbi
sour colocasia
Tamil Nadu

Preparation time	10 minutes
Cooking time	40 minutes
Serves	4–6

Coconut (sliced)	¼
Colocasia	500 gm
Vegetable oil	2 tbsp
Mustard seeds (brown)	1tsp
Curry leaves	6–8
Onion (chopped)	2 (medium)
Green chilli (finely chopped)	2
Tomato (chopped)	1 (medium)
Tamarind pulp	1 tbsp
Salt	To taste (1 tsp)
Water (if required)	2 tbsp

Put the sliced coconut in a blender and make a coarse paste. Keep aside.

Wash, clean and boil the colocasia with skin for about 15 minutes or till tender. Cool, peel and cut it into thick slices.

Heat oil in a pan, add the mustard seeds and curry leaves. They will crackle at once. Immediately put in the chopped onion and green chilli and fry till the onions are soft.

Now add the chopped tomatoes and stir for 6–8 minutes. When the tomatoes are well mixed with the onions, add the tamarind pulp, salt and coconut. In place of tomatoes, one tablespoon of curd can be used if so desired. Cook for 5–7minutes.

Next, add the boiled colocasia and mix thoroughly. If required, add water so that it does not get stuck at the bottom of the pan. Cover and cook it on a slow fire for another 5 minutes.

Transfer to a serving dish, scraping the mixture thoroughly from the pan. Serve with chapattis.

khatta mitha kaddoo
sweet and sour pumpkin
Uttar Pradesh

Preparation time	15 minutes
Cooking time	45 minutes
Serves	4

Vegetable oil	3 tbsp
Cumin seeds	½ tsp
Onion seeds	¼ tsp
Onion (chopped)	2 (medium)
Ginger (chopped)	1"
Turmeric powder	½ tsp
Chilli powder	½ tsp
Salt	To taste (1 tsp)
Tomato (chopped)	2 (medium)
Red pumpkin	750 gm
(deseeded, peeled,	
and cut into ½" pieces)	
Brown sugar/Jaggery	1 tbsp
Mango powder	2½ tsp
Garam masala	½ tsp

Heat the oil in a medium pan, then add the cumin and onion seeds. They will crackle immediately.

Now add the sliced onion and ginger, lower the heat and fry the onion for 5–7 minutes until it is soft and transparent.

Add the turmeric powder, chilli powder, salt and chopped tomatoes. Stir and fry till the tomatoes are soft.

Add the pumpkin, mix well, then cover and cook on a slow fire till the pumpkin is soft and tender. Add the sugar, and mango powder and mix well. Do not worry if a few pieces of pumpkin get mashed as this will give proper consistency to the dish. Sprinkle garam masala and cook for few minutes.

Serve hot with paratha or chapattis with yellow lentil.

sambhar
yellow lentil with vegetables
Tamil Nadu

Preparation time	30–35 minute
Cooking time	40 minutes
Serves	4

Yellow lentil	1 cup
Okra	½ cup
(cut into 1" size, or any other non-starch vegetable)	
Drumstick	2
(cut into 2" long)	
Aubergine/Brinjal	1 (small)
(1" dice)	
Water	4–5 cups
Turmeric powder	1 tsp
Chilli powder	1 tsp
Onion (sliced)	1 cup
Tomato (sliced)	2 (medium)
Green chilli	3–4
(sliced lengthwise)	
Salt	To taste (2 tsp)
Vegetable oil	3 tbsp
Mustard seeds	1 tsp
Fenugreek seeds	½ tsp
Cumin seeds	2 tsp
Coriander seeds	1 tsp
White lentil (washed)	1 tbsp
Sesame seeds	1 tsp
Curry leaves	10–12
Asafoetida	⅓ tsp
Tamarind pulp	1 tbsp
Jaggery	1 tbsp
Coconut paste	6 tbsp
Green coriander (chopped)	2 tbsp

Put the washed and drained lentil in a thick-bottomed saucepan or pressure cooker. Add the vegetables, water, turmeric powder, chilli powder, onion, tomatoes, green chillies and salt till the lentil is tender. Mix one tablespoon of oil and set aside.

Heat the remaining oil in a big saucepan or kadahi, and add mustard seeds, fenugreek seeds, cumin, coriander seeds, white lentil and sesame seeds. Fry until the seeds start crackling.

Now add the curry leaves and asafoetida, and stir for a while.

Transfer the cooked lentil into the pan. Add the tamarind pulp and cook for 5–7 minutes. Next add the jaggery and coconut paste and boil for 5–6 minutes.

Now add the chopped coriander and serve hot. Usually it is served with dosa, idli, or vada but goes well with steamed rice also.

dal phooli
lemon flavoured dry lentil

Andhra Pradesh

Preparation time	10–15 minutes
Cooking time	25–30 minutes
Serves	4–6

Vegetable oil	2 tbsp
Mustard seeds	1 tsp
Curry leaves	8–10
Onion (chopped)	1 (medium)
Ginger (chopped)	1 tsp
Garlic (chopped)	1 clove
Turmeric powder	1 tsp
Red chilli powder	1 tsp
Salt	To taste (1½ tsp)
Green coriander (chopped)	1 tbsp
Red lentils (washed and soaked)	1 cup
Lemon zest (optional)	1 tsp (scrape the lemon in a nut grater)
Water	1¼ cup
Lemon juice	1 lemon
Green chilli (chopped)	2

Heat oil in a saucepan. Add the mustard seeds. As soon as they crackle add the curry leaves and stir for a minute.

Now add the onion, ginger and garlic and fry till the onions are transparent and golden in colour.

Next, add turmeric powder, chilli powder, salt and chopped coriander, and fry for 5–6 minutes.

Add the washed lentil and lemon zest. Add water, mix well and cover, cook for 20 minutes on a slow fire or till the lentil is tender and the water is absorbed.

Pour the lemon juice and stir well. Cover and leave it to simmer for 3–4 minutes. Transfer to a serving dish and serve with chapattis. It is a good accompaniment to any main dish.

cholar dal
bengal gram with coconut
West Bengal

Preparation time	10 minutes
Cooking time	50–55 minutes
Serves	6–8

Water	4–5 cups
Bengal gram (split)	1 cup
Bay leaf	1
Turmeric powder	1 tsp
Chilli powder	½ tsp
Coriander powder	1 tsp
Cumin powder	1 tsp
Green chilli	4
Sultanas/Raisins (washed and soaked)	1 tbsp
Salt	To taste (2 tsp)
Sugar	2 tsp
Ghee	2 tbsp
Cumin seeds	1 tsp
Dried red chilli (whole)	3–4
Coconut (coarsely grated)	¼
Garam masala	1½ tsp

Boil water in a saucepan or pressure cooker. Add washed and drained lentil along with bay leaf, turmeric powder, chilli powder, coriander powder and cumin powder. Cook for 35–40 minutes (in a saucepan) or 8–10 minutes (in pressure cooker) until the lentil is nearly done.

Add the sultanas/raisins, salt and sugar. Mix well and continue cooking till the lentil is tender. Now put the ghee in a saucepan and heat it. When the ghee is fairly hot, add the cumin seeds and dry red chilli. As soon as it starts crackling add the grated coconut and fry till brown.

Pour this over the lentil and mix well. Cover and let it simmer for 5–6 minutes on a slow fire.

Sprinkle garam masala powder and stir well. Remove from fire and transfer to a serving dish. Serve with lucchi or plain rice.

bagare baigan
tempered aubergine
Hyderabad

Preparation time	20 minutes
Cooking time	40 minutes
Serves	4

Baby aubergine/Brinjal	10–12
Refined vegetable oil	5 tbsp
Onion (chopped)	2 (medium)
Fresh ginger (finely chopped)	1½ "
Garlic (thinly sliced)	3 cloves
Sesame seeds	2 tsp
Poppy seeds	2 tsp
Peanuts (shelled)	2 tbsp
Cumin seeds	1½ tsp
Coriander seeds	1½ tbsp
Red chilli (whole, dry)	3 (medium)
Coconut (grated)	3 tbsp
Fenugreek seeds	½ tsp
Curry leaves	6–8
Salt	To taste (2 tsp)
Tamarind pulp	1 tsp
Water	¾ cup (to requirement)

Wash dry and slit the aubergines lengthwise carefully so that they are held by the stalk. Heat 4 tbsp oil in a deep frying pan and fry the aubergines with care so that they do not break from the stalk.

When fried from all sides, remove from the pan (draining the oil completely) and keep aside.

Make a smooth paste of the chopped onion, ginger, garlic, sesame seeds, poppy seeds, peanuts, ½ tsp cumin seeds, coriander seeds, red chilli and grated coconut through a blender or a food processor. If needed, 1–2 tbsp water can be added.

Heat the remaining 1 tbsp oil in the pan. Add ½ tsp cumin seeds and fenugreek seeds. When they start crackling add the curry leaves. At once add the onion, peanut mixture and salt. Fry the mixture in the pan for about 10–12 minutes till the oil separates. Water should be added to avoid dryness and sticking to the pan.

Add the tamarind and cook for a few minutes. Add the fried aubergines and cover with a lid. Cook the aubergines with the mixture for another 15 minutes. Serve hot.

gatta curry
gram flour dumplings
Rajasthan

Preparation time	25 minutes
Cooking time	40 minutes
Serves	4

Gram flour	1 cup
Chilli powder	2½ tsp
Salt	To taste (2 tsp)
Vegetable oil	6 tbsp
Water	2 cups
Cumin seeds	1 tsp
Fenugreek seeds	½ tsp
Curd/Yoghurt	½ cup
Turmeric powder	1 tsp
Coriander powder	4 tsp
Asafoetida	½ tsp
Garam masala	½ tsp
Mango powder	1 tsp
Green coriander (chopped)	3 tbsp

Sieve the gram flour and add 1 tsp chilli powder, ½ tsp salt and 2 tbsp oil and make a hard dough. If required add a little more oil. Roll into 4–5" long strips, 1" diameter. Boil these strips for 10–12 minutes in water till they become hard. Cool, cut into 1 cm. round slices and keep aside. These are known as gattas.

Heat the remaining oil in a pan, then add the cumin and fenugreek seeds. They start crackling immediately.

Now add the beaten curd and all the remaining spices except the mango powder and chopped coriander. Add water and cook for 10–12 minutes.

When the gravy starts leaving the oil, add the boiled gattas and mango powder. Stir thoroughly and cook for another few minutes. Remove from fire, transfer to a serving dish and sprinkle chopped coriander. Serve hot with boiled rice.

bandhakopir tarkari
cabbage and potato curry
West Bengal

Preparation time	15 minutes
Cooking time	15–20 minutes
Serves	4–6

Mustard oil	4 tbsp
Potato (cut into 1"x8" dices)	2 (medium)
Cabbage (finely shredded)	1 (approx. 500 gm)
Bay leaf	2
Salt	To taste (1 tsp)
Green chilli	3–4
Chilli powder	1½ tsp
Turmeric powder	1 tsp
Cumin powder	1 tsp
Coriander powder	1½ tsp
Ginger (julienne)	1 tbsp
Garam masala	1 tsp
Sugar	¾ tsp

Heat mustard oil in a kadahi or a wok to smoking point. Fry the diced potatoes till golden brown.

Add the shredded cabbage, bay leaves, and salt, cover and let it simmer for 7–8 minutes on a low fire.

Now add the chilli, turmeric, cumin and coriander powder. Stir well to mix the spices with the cabbage well. Cover and cook for another 7–8 minutes. Cabbage and potatoes will be cooked in their own water.

Remove lid, add the ginger julienne and sugar. Stir well so that the spices don't get burnt at the bottom of the kadahi. Cook till the potatoes are tender and the cabbage is soft. If required, 1 tbsp water can be added.

Scrape well from the bottom of the kadahi and transfer to a serving bowl. Sprinkle garam masala and keep it covered. Serve with chapattis or parathas.

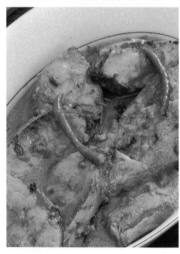

fish and

shellfish

know your ingredients

Carom Seeds (Ajwain)

Carom seeds are spices with digestive properties, often used to give relief from minor stomach aches and with foods that cause flatulence. It has small, distinctive light brown seeds.

Curry Leaves (Curry Patta, Meetha Neem)

Thin, shiny, dark green leaves with the distinct 'curry' flavour of the commercially produced 'curry powder.' Mainly used in south and west Indian cooking. Best when lightly fried in hot oil for a few seconds.

Green Chillies (Hari Mirch)

Fresh chillies should be firm and shiny. They are often eaten raw with meals and are burning hot. If you just want the flavour, slit the chilli, remove the seeds, and rub a little salt inside. Then wash thoroughly. Remember to wash your hands after handling chillies and don't touch your eyes.

machhi amritsari
masala fried fish
Punjab

Preparation time	30–40 minutes
Cooking time	10–15 minutes
Serves	4–6

Fish (any white, firm fish, preferably river fish)	1 kg
Gram flour	1 cup
Carom seeds	2 tbsp
Ginger paste	2 tbsp
Garlic paste	2 tbsp
Salt	To taste (2 tsp)
Red chilli powder	2 tsp
Kashmiri chilli powder	1 tsp
Turmeric powder	1 tsp
Pepper powder (white)	1/2 tsp
Refined oil	To deep fry
Chaat masala	2 tsp

Clean, wash and cut fish into 1/2" darnes. Pat dry the fish with a cloth and keep aside.

Dry-roast the gram flour to light brown and carom seeds to golden brown.

Mix together ginger and garlic paste, salt, chilli powder, Kashmiri chilli powder, turmeric powder, carom seeds and white pepper powder.

Now mix the roasted gram flour and add 5–6 tbsp water to make a paste of coating consistency. Generously apply the paste to the fish darnes on all sides and leave to marinate for 25–30 minutes.

Heat refined oil in a kadahi. Fry the fish on medium heat, a few pieces at a time until crisp. Serve hot, sprinkled with chaat masala. It can be served as a snack or even as part of a main meal.

doi maachh
fish cooked with curd
West Bengal

Refined oil	3 tbsp
Bay leaf	2
Onion (finely chopped)	2 (medium)
Ginger paste	2 tsp
Turmeric powder	½ tsp
Red chilli powder	2 tsp
Water	1 cup
Curd/Yoghurt	½ cup
Salt	To taste (1½ tsp)
Sugar	1 tsp
Green chilli (slit)	4
Rahu fish (or any white fish)	6–8 pieces (approx. 600 gm)
Garam masala	1 tsp

Preparation time	20–25 minutes
Cooking time	30–35 minutes
Serves	4

Heat the refined oil in a heavy base saucepan, then add the bay leaf and chopped onion. Fry the onion until it is golden brown in colour.

Add ginger paste, turmeric, and chilli powder, and 1 tbsp water if masala sticks to the pan. Mix the curd well with water and pour into the pan, straining through a sieve. Let it simmer for 6–8 minutes.

Add salt, sugar and green chillies, and let it simmer for another 3–4 minutes.

Put cleaned, washed and wiped fish pieces in the pan very carefully. Cook until the fish is cooked well and the gravy has thickened, separating from the oil.

Sprinkle garam masala and cover the pan. Serve hot with plain boiled rice or pulao.

goan fish curry
fish curry goan style
Goa

Preparation time	30 minutes
Cooking time	15–20 minutes
Serves	4–6

Pomfret (or any white fish)	800 gm–1kg
Ginger	2"
Garlic	3–4 cloves
Tamarind	2 tbsp (approx. 50 gm)
Red chilli (dry)	10 (small)
Coriander seeds	2 tbsp
Cumin seeds	2 tsp
Turmeric	1 tsp
Water	2 cups
Refined oil	4 tbsp
Onion (sliced)	1 (large)
Tomato (chopped)	1
Coconut milk	1 cup
Salt	To taste (1 tsp)
Green chilli	4

Clean, wash and cut the fish into darnes or steaks. Peel and chop ginger and garlic. De-seed tamarind if it is with seeds.

Put together ginger, garlic, tamarind, red chilli, coriander and cumin seeds and turmeric. Add about 5lb water and make a fine paste.

Heat the refined oil in a handi or saucepan. Add sliced onion and fry till golden brown. Next, add chopped tomatoes and fry for 3–4 minutes.

Now put in the ginger, garlic and spice paste and fry for 3–4 minutes.

Add 1½ cups of water and half of the coconut milk. Boil for 2 minutes, then add the pieces of fish and let them simmer on low heat for 5–6 minutes.

Finally, add salt, the remaining coconut milk, stir well and boil for another 2 minutes or until the fish is cooked.

Gently transfer to a serving bowl and sprinkle green chilli on top. Serve hot with boiled rice.

chingri jhal
spicy prawn
Orissa

Preparation time	15 minutes
Cooking time	25 minutes
Serves	4

Prawn	500 gm
Ginger	1"
Garlic	2 cloves
Mustard seeds	1 tbsp
Mustard oil	2–3 tbsp
(refined oil can be used)	
Turmeric powder	1 tsp
Red chilli powder	½ tsp
Salt	To taste
	(approx. ½ tsp)
Green chilli	3

Shell, devein the prawns. Remove the heads if so desired. The authentic preparation is with the heads on.

In a blender grind ginger, garlic and mustard seeds into a smooth paste. Add 2 tbsp water, if required.

Heat the oil in a frying pan or kadahi till it reaches smoking point. Add the ginger-garlic paste and other dry spices, then add the green chilli and cook for 3–4 minutes.

Water can be added to make it into coating consistency.

Add the prawn and cook for 4–5 minutes. Add salt and serve hot. Usually eaten with plain boiled rice.

fish caldine
yellow fish curry
Goa

Preparation time	25 minutes
Cooking time	30 minutes
Serves	4

Fresh coconut (grated)	½
Ginger	1" piece
Garlic	3 cloves
Cumin seeds	½ tsp
Turmeric powder	1 tsp
Pomfret	1 (350–400 gm)
Refined oil	2 tbsp
Green chilli (slit lengthwise)	2–3
Onion (chopped)	1 onion
Tamarind (pulp)	20 gm/1tbsp
Salt	To taste (1 tsp)
Green coriander (chopped)	1 tbsp

Soak the grated coconut in one cup of hot water. When cool, pass through a blender, strain and set aside the coconut milk.

Add one more cup of warm water to the coconut pulp along with ginger, garlic, cumin and turmeric. Put this mixture into the blender and blend it for 2–3 minutes. Remove, strain through a sieve and set aside the thin mixture.

Cut the fish into slices, wash and pat dry.

Heat the refined oil in a sauce pan and fry the onion till golden brown. Add both the strained mixtures and bring to boil.

Add the fish and cook for 8–10 minutes or till it is done.

Finally, add the tamarind pulp, sliced green chilli and salt. Cook for a few minutes. Sprinkle chopped green coriander just before removing from the fire. Serve hot with rice.

sas machhi
parsi style fish
Maharashtra

Preparation time	25 minutes
Cooking time	35 minutes
Serves	4

Pomfret/Sole (any white fish fillet)	600 gm
Red chilli (dry)	4 (small)
Cumin seeds	1 tsp
Garlic	2–3 cloves
Refined oil	2 tbsp
Onion (chopped)	2 (medium)
Tomato (chopped)	2 (medium)
Water	2 cups
Salt	To taste (1 tsp)
Sugar	1 tsp
Green coriander (chopped)	3 sprigs
Lemon juice	1 tsp
Eggs	2
White vinegar (optional)	2 tbsp
Black pepper (crushed)	½ tsp

Wash the fish and cut into thick slices 1" thick.

Make a smooth paste of chilli, cumin seeds and garlic in a blender. If needed, add a little water.

Heat oil in a pan. Put the chopped onion in it and fry till it is golden brown.
Add the cumin garlic paste and fry for a few more minutes.

Add the chopped tomatoes and fry till the oil separates from the mixture. If the mixture sticks to the bottom of the pan, add a little water (1–2 tbsp) and continue frying.

Add the remaining water. Bring to the boil, reduce heat and cook for 7–8 minutes. Add salt, sugar and chopped coriander.

Add the fish and cover. Cook till the fish is tender (approximately 10 minutes). Sprinkle lemon juice and remove and set aside. Remove the lid.

Lightly whip the eggs with vinegar and crushed pepper. Add the egg mixture gently in the fish (after the steam has left it).
Fold in gently, cover and cook on slow fire for 4–5 minutes or till the egg mixture has thickened. The mixture should not be boiled as the egg may curdle. Remove and serve hot wish plain boiled rice.

konju masala
spicy prawn curry
Kerala

Preparation time	20 minutes
Cooking time	20 minutes
Serves	4

Red chilli (dry, soaked in water)	4
Black peppercorn	2 tsp
Cumin seeds	1 tsp
Ginger (chopped)	2 tsp
Garlic (chopped)	2 tsp
Turmeric powder	1/2 tsp
Prawns (shelled and deveined)	500 gm (small)
Refined oil	1/3 cup
Mustard seeds (brown)	1/2 tsp
Curry leaves	12–14
Onion (sliced)	2 (medium)
Tamarind pulp (soaked in 2 cups water and strained)	2 1/2 tbsp
Salt	To taste (3/4 tsp)

Grind the dry red chillies, black peppercorns, cumin seeds, ginger and garlic in a blender to a smooth paste. If necessary, add one or two tablespoons of water.

Mix this paste with turmeric powder and add the washed and dried prawns. Coat the prawns with the paste thoroughly and set aside.

Now, in a medium saucepan, heat the oil. Put in the mustard seeds and curry leaves. As soon as the seeds starts popping, add the sliced onion and cook till brown in colour.

Next, add the marinated prawns and stir for 2–3 minutes. Add the strained tamarind pulp and salt. Bring to a boil, lower the heat and let is simmer for 6–8 minutes till the prawns are cooked.

Serve hot with plain boiled rice.

sorse maach
mustard fish

West Bengal

Rahu (or any white firm fish)	500 gm
Mustard oil	4–5 tbsp
Yellow mustard seeds	2 tbsp
Ginger	1–1½"
Green chilli (deseeded)	2
Water	500 ml
Onion seeds	½ tsp
Turmeric powder	1 tsp
Red chilli powder	½ tsp
Salt	To taste

Preparation time	20 minutes
Cooking time	25 minutes
Serves	4

Wash fish and pat dry. Cut into pieces as per requirement.

Heat the mustard oil to smoking point. Add a few pieces of fish at a time, fry for 5–7 minutes till light golden brown and keep aside.

Keep the remaining oil for sauce.
Put the mustard seeds, ginger, chilli and approximately 100 ml water in a blender and grind to a very fine smooth paste. Re-heat the pan with the remaining oil. Add onion seeds, and when they start popping add mustard paste, turmeric powder and chilli powder.

Add the remaining water and salt and give a good boil for 5–7 minutes.

Add the fried fish and simmer for another five minutes, coverning the pan with a lid. Transfer to a dish. Sprinkle a few slit green chillies (optional).

meen malabar curry
fish curry kerala style
Kerala

Preparation time	15 minutes
Cooking time	40 minutes
Serves	4

Fresh coconut (grated)	1½
Red chilli (dry)	10–12 (small)
Tomato (sliced)	1 (medium)
Sole/Bekti or any white fish (filleted and cubed)	500 gm
Salt	To taste (2 tsp)
Coconut oil	3 tbsp
Water	4–5 cups
Raw mango (peeled, deseeded and diced)	2 (medium)
Green chilli (slit)	6
Ginger (julienne)	2 tbsp
Curry leaves	15–18
Onion (chopped)	2 (medium)

Grind the grated coconut, dry red chilli and tomato to a fine paste in a blender or food processor.

Clean, wash and pat dry the fish, sprinkle a little salt and coconut oil and set aside.

Take a big saucepan, mix water with the coconut paste and boil for about 20 minutes till the water is reduced and the coconut paste is well blended.

Now add raw mangoes, green chillies, ginger and curry leaves. Cook for 7–8 minutes. Add the fish and salt. Let it simmer for 5–6 minutes, covered.

In a frying pan put 2 tbsp coconut oil and heat it to smoking point. Fry the chopped onion till golden brown.

Add the fried onion to the fish. Cover and let it simmer for 3–4 minutes until the fish is soaked.

Serve hot with steamed or boiled rice.

methiwaali machhi
spicy fish with fenugreek
Himachal Pradesh

Preparation time	35–40 minutes
Cooking time	35–40 minutes
Serves	6

Fish fillet (any white firm fish)	1 kg
Lemon juice	1 lemon
Salt	To taste (2 tsp)
Onion (sliced)	1 (medium)
Ginger (chopped)	1 tsp
Garlic (chopped)	3 cloves
Red chilli (dry)	4
Fenugreek seeds	½ tsp
Coriander seeds	2 tsp
Cumin seeds	1 tsp
Turmeric powder	¾ tsp
Refined oil	3 tbsp
Yoghurt/Curd	½ cup
Fresh fenugreek (chopped)	½ cup

Clean, wash and cut the fish into 2 inch cubes, pat dry. Rub with lemon juice and 1 tsp salt. Keep aside.

Put onion, ginger, garlic, dry whole red chilli, and fenugreek, coriander and cumin seeds, and turmeric in a blender. Blend to a smooth paste adding 2–3 tbsps of water. Keep aside.

Heat refined oil in a sauce pan. Add onion paste in it and fry for 6–8 minutes. Beat the yoghurt well and put in the onion mixture. Add the chopped fresh fenugreek. Fry the mixture until golden brown and oil separates from the mixture. Slide the fish pieces very gently in the pan. Cook uncovered in low fire for 10–12 minutes, stirring occasionally and gently, not to break the fish pieces or until the fish is cooked.

Serve with steamed/boiled rice.

machhi ka soola
grilled fish kabab
Rajasthan

Preparation time	40–45 minutes
Cooking time	20 minutes
Serves	6

Fish fillet (Sole or any white firm fish)	1 kg
Refined oil	3 tbsp
Onion (sliced)	1 (medium)
Garlic (peeled)	3 cloves
Ginger (sliced)	1"
Chilli powder	2 tsp
Turmeric powder	1 tsp
Carom seeds	1 tsp
Salt	To taste (2 tsp)
Green coriander (chopped)	1 tbsp
Lemon juice	1 lemon

Remove bones from the fish if there is any with the sharp point of knife. Clean, wash and cut the fish into 2" dice.

Heat the refined oil in a small frying pan. Fry the sliced onion and one clove remaining garlic to pale golden brown colour. Remove the onion and garlic from oil. Put in blender with ginger remaining and blend to a fine paste. If needed add 1–2 tbs of water. Mix the chilli powder, turmeric powder, carom seeds, salt, chopped coriander, lemon juice and remaining oil with the paste. Rub the mixture on all sides of the fish pieces. Leave to marinate for 10–15 minutes.

Light a charcoal grill or preheat oven to 175°C. Take a skewer and thread the fish pieces into it (3 to 4 pieces in one skewer). Cook the fish on fire or in oven rotating regularly to cook evenly.

Serve hot with parathas and salad.

mysore fish curry
a south indian speciality
Karnataka

Preparation time	20 minutes
Cooking time	25–30 minutes
Serves	4–6

Mackerel/Herring/Trout	12–14
Salt	To taste (2 tsp)
Tamarind pulp	1 tbsp
Coconut (grated)	½ cup
Red chilli (dry)	4–6
Black peppercorn	4–6
Refined oil	2 tbsp
Garlic (chopped)	4 cloves
Curry leaves	10–12
Green chilli (slit lengthwise)	2–3

Clean the fish. Remove the head and wash inside the stomach, drain and pat dry with a kitchen paper or cloth. Smear 1 tsp salt and set aside.

In a blender, make a fine paste with tamarind, grated coconut, dried red chilli and black peppercorn by adding 2 tbsp of water.

Heat the refined oil in a saucepan. Add chopped garlic and curry leaves and fry for 1–2 minutes.

Now add the coconut and tamarind paste and fry for 2–3 minutes, adding water to form a thick, pouring gravy. Cook for 4–5 minutes.

Put in the fish and cover, lower the heat and simmer for 6–8 minutes till the fish is cooked. Stir gently, adding salt and green chilli. Lift the fish first with a slicer to a serving dish, then pour the gravy on top. Serve with plain boiled rice.

bhetki paturi
bhetki fish cooked in banana leaves
West Bengal

Preparation time	20–25 minutes
Cooking time	30–35 minutes
Serves	6–8

Yellow mustard seeds	3 tbsp
Green chilli	6–8
Water	4–5 tbsp
Bhetki fish fillet	900 gm–1 kg
(cut into 3–4" pieces, cleaned and washed)	
Turmeric powder	1 tsp
Chilli powder	1 tsp
Salt	To taste (1½ tsp)
Banana leaves (halved)	6–8
(Aluminium foil can be used instead of banana leaves but the flavour will be different)	
Mustard oil	3–4 tbsp

Make a fine paste of the mustard seeds and 2 green chillies adding the water.

Place the fish pieces on a medium size plate. Add the mustard paste, turmeric powder, chilli powder and salt. Mix the masala mixtures and the fish thoroughly but carefully so that the fish does not break. Keep for 8–10 minutes.

On an iron griddle or tawa, place the banana leaves crosswise alternately. Gently place the fish pieces in the centre of the banana leaves. Put mustard oil on top. Make sure that they do not overlap. It will be worth cooking it in 2–3 batches.

Put the coated masala in the fish and remaining slit green chilli. Fold the banana leaves from all sides like an envelop and make a square packet. Tie with a string if necessary. Put the tawa on the fire and cook for 15–18 minutes.

To serve, place the packet in a platter and undo the string only before serving. Serve with plain boiled rice.

prawn balchao

Goa

Preparation time	20 minutes
Cooking time	25–30 minutes
Serves	4–6

Prawns (shelled)	500 gms (medium)
Cumin seeds	1 tsp
Black peppercorn	1 tsp
Red chilli (dry)	6–8
White vinegar	2 tbsp
Turmeric powder	1 tsp
Refined oil	3 tbsp
Onion (minced)	3 (medium)
Ginger (chopped)	1 tsp
Garlic (chopped)	3 cloves
Curry leaves	10–12
Salt	To taste (1 tsp)
Malt vinegar	1 tbsp
Green chilli (deseeded and chopped)	4–5

Devein, clean and wash the prawns. Grind together cumin seeds, black peppercorn and dry red chilli in white vinegar to a fine paste. Mix turmeric powder in it and keep aside.

Heat oil in a thick bottom pan and fry the minced onion until golden brown. Add the ground spice and fry for 4–5 minutes. Add the prawns and cook for 6–8 minutes until the prawns are well blended with spices. Add chopped ginger, garlic, curry leaves, green chillies, salt and malt vinegar. Stir well. Simmer in low fire till the prawns are well cooked.

Adjust seasoning and transfer to serving dish. Serve with rice. Avoid reheating as this may affect the texture of the prawns.

chicken

know your ingredients

Fenugreek (Methi Dana or Methre)

Another versatile plant in which the fresh leaves are used as a herb
and the seeds as the spice. Fenugreek seeds are very bitter, so they
should be fried until dark brown in colour to help remove some of
the bitterness. It is best to literally burn them, then cool and strain
the oil, discard the bitter seeds and use the flavoured oil.

Poppy Seeds (Khus khus)

Tiny, cream-coloured seeds with a slight taste of the nuts, which
have a cooling effect when ground and used. The seeds are used
in savoury dishes as well as in sweets. Also acts as a thickener.

Black Pepper (Kali Mirch)

This is a traditional ingredient in the preparation of medicine in the
Indian Ayurvedic system. A digestive and stimulant, it also enhances
the flavour of any dish to which it is added. Generally regarded as
a 'warm' spice, it is an essential ingredient of Garam Masala.

murg makhanwala
butter chicken
Delhi

Preparation time	10–15 minutes
Cooking time	35 minutes
Serves	4–5

Ginger (coarsely chopped)	1"
Tomato	6 (medium)
Green chilli	1
Onion (sliced)	1 (medium)
Vegetable oil	3 tbsp
Chicken	1 (cut into 8 pieces)
Cumin powder	1 tsp
Chilli powder	1 tsp
Water	1 cup
Salt	To taste (1 tsp)
Butter	2 tbsp
Cream	½ cup
Green coriander (chopped)	4–5 sprigs
Garam masala	¾ tsp

Put chopped ginger, tomatoes, green chilli and onion in a blender and make a smooth paste.

Heat the vegetable oil in a heavy bottomed pan. Fry the chicken pieces 4–5 at a time for 10–15 minutes to golden colour. Set aside.

Reduce the heat, add the cumin and red chilli powder and stir for a few seconds. Now add the blended tomato mixture, water and cook for 15–20 minutes.

Add the chicken pieces and salt. Cook till the chicken is tender.

Lower heat and add the butter and cream. Cook on a slow fire for 5–7 minutes.

Sprinkle garam masala powder and chopped green coriander. Do not boil after adding cream as it may curdle.

sambalpuri murg

chicken curry from sambalpur

Orissa

Preparation time	20 minutes
Cooking time	40 minutes
Serves	4

Onion	3 (medium)
Green chilli	2
Vegetable oil	4–5 tbsp
Bay leaf	2
Chicken (Cut into 8 pieces)	1 (1–1.5 kg)
Salt	To taste (1½ tsp)
Water	200 ml (100 ml if using pressure cooker)
Dry red chilli	2 (medium)
Turmeric powder	1 tsp
Fresh coconut (grated)	½
Ginger paste	1 tsp
Garlic paste	1 tsp

Place the onion and green chilli in a blender and make a smooth paste. Heat half of the oil in a heavy base pan or pressure cooker.

Add the bay leaves and chicken pieces. Put in the onion paste, salt and water. Cover and cook for 25–30 minutes till the chicken is tender and the liquid has evaporated. Lift the chicken pieces, scraping the sauce from it. Leave the sauce in the pan.

Heat the remaining oil in a pan. Fry the chicken pieces for 10–12 minutes until golden in colour. Keep aside.

Put the ginger and garlic paste, dry red chilli, turmeric powder and grated coconut in the previous remaining oil, fry for 7–10 minutes till the coconut is golden brown in colour and the oil has separated.

Add the fried chicken pieces, coat them in the sauce and cook for 3–5 minutes. Serve hot with boiled rice.

handi murg
spicy chicken

Preparation time	40–45 minutes
Cooking time	45 minutes–1 hr
Serves	4–6

Chicken (cut into desired small pieces)	1 (approx. 900 gm)
Refined oil	6–7 tbsp
Onion (sliced)	4–5
Green chilli	3
Ginger (chopped)	1½ tsp
Garlic	3–4 cloves
Green cardamom	3–4
Cinnamon	2"stick
Tomato (chopped)	1 cup
Red chilli powder	2 tsp
Coriander powder	1 tsp
Turmeric powder	1 tsp
Salt	To taste (2 tsp)
Water	1 cup
Green coriander (chopped)	1 tbsp
Mace	1 flower

Clean and wash the chicken pieces thoroughly and keep aside to drain and dry.

In a saucepan put 5 tbsp refined oil and heat to smoking point. Fry the sliced onions a little at a time to golden brown and spread on to a kitchen paper or towel to get dry and crispy.

Then, take all the fried onions and make a fine paste in a blender with green chilli, ginger and garlic. If required add a few spoons of water to get a fine smooth paste.

Add 2 tbsp refined oil in the remaining oil in the saucepan. Add mace, green cardamom, cloves and cinnamom stick. Next put in the chicken pieces and fry for 4–5 minutes.

Now add chopped tomatoes and fry them till they are totally mashed and well blended with the chicken pieces.

Next, add the red chilli, coriander and turmeric powder. Cook for 3–4 minutes. Now add the brown onion paste and mix well with the chicken. Fry for 4–5 minutes till the mixture separates from the oil. Finally, add salt and water, stir well, cover and cook for 8–10 minutes or until the chicken is tender. Sprinkle chopped coriander and cover for 2 minutes. Serve with naan or paratha.

salli murg

parsi chicken with straw potatoes

Maharashtra

Preparation time	35 minutes
Cooking time	45–55 minutes
Serves	4

Refined oil	3 tbsp
Onion (thinly sliced)	2 (medium)
Green chilli (sliced)	2
Ginger–garlic paste	1 tbsp
Turmeric powder	½ tsp
Chilli powder	¾ tsp
Tomato (chopped)	3 (medium)
Chicken	1 (900 gm–1 kg)
(cut into small pieces)	
Salt	To taste (1 tsp)
Sugar	1 tsp
Apricot (dried)	6
Garam masala	½ tsp
Green coriander	2 tbsp
(chopped)	

For salli (straw potatoes)

Potato	4–5 (medium)
(peeled and cut into very fine julienne)	
Refined oil	To fry
Salt	1 tsp

Take a heavy base saucepan and heat 3 tbsp oil. Fry the onions until golden brown. Add the green chilli, ginger–garlic paste, turmeric and chilli powder and stir-fry for 4–5 minutes.

Now add the chopped tomatoes and cook, stirring continuously till the tomatoes are soft and pulpy.

Next, add the chicken pieces and fry till the moisture around the chicken dries up. Add salt, sugar and water just enough to cover the surface of the chicken. Let it simmer for 15–20 minutes until the oil separates from the sauce.

Add roughly chopped apricot and cook till the chicken is tender.

In the meantime prepare potato straws. Peel and cut them in thin stripes. Wash in cold water and pat dry the julienne potatoes. Drop fry in very hot oil until crisp and golden.

Drain and sprinkle salt. Keep aside. To finish the chicken, sprinkle garam masala and chopped coriander on top. The salli or straw potatoes are put on just before serving to prevent them from becoming soft.

murg kata masala
chicken with fried spices
Uttar Pradesh

Preparation time	20–25 minutes
Cooking time	45 minutes
Serve	4–6

Refined oil	5 tbsp
Bay leaf	2
Black pepper (whole)	1 tsp
Cardamom (black)	3
Cloves	½ tsp
Cinnamon	2″ stick
Whole coriander seeds	1 tbsp
Red chilli (dry)	4–6
Onion (sliced)	4 (medium)
Ginger–garlic paste	1 tbsp
Chicken (cut into 12 pieces)	1 (approx. 800–900 gm)
Curd/Yoghurt	½ cup
Yellow chilli powder	½ tsp
Salt	To taste (1½ tsp)

Take a heavy base pan or pressure cooker. If using a pressure cooker, the cooking time will be much less. Heat the refined oil in the pan. Put all the whole spices in the oil and fry for 2–3 minutes.

Add the sliced onions and fry till they are soft and transparent.

Now add the ginger-garlic paste and fry for 3–4 minutes. Make sure the onions don't get browned or even light brown.

Add the chicken pieces and fry for 5–7 minutes.

Next add the curd (beaten well) and yellow chilli powder. Stir for 5–7 minutes so that the curd is well mixed with the chicken.

Add salt, mix thoroughly, cover with a lid and cook on a low fire till the chicken is tender and has absorbed most of the moisture. Mix it thoroughly and leave it to simmer, covering the pan, for 2–3 minutes.

Check the seasoning before transferring to a serving dish. Serve hot with roomali roti or naan.

dhaniya murg
coriander chicken

Madhya Pradesh

Preparation time	35 minute
Cooking time	40 minutes
Serves	4–6

Refined oil	5–6 tbsp
Cardamom (black)	2
Cumin seeds	½ tsp
Onion (chopped)	3 (medium)
Chicken (cut into 12 pieces)	1 whole (approx. 800–900gm)
Ginger paste	1 tbsp
Garlic paste	2 tsp
Red chilli powder	1 tsp
Coriander powder	2 tsp
Turmeric powder	¾ tsp
Tomato (chopped)	3 (medium)
Green chilli (chopped)	1 tbsp
Green coriander (chopped)	1½ cup
Salt	To taste
Water	1½ cup
Garam masala	½ tsp

Heat the refined oil in a heavy pan or pressure cooker. Add black cardamom and cumin seeds. When the seeds starts crackling add the chopped onions and fry for 4–5 minutes till they are soft.

Now add the chicken pieces (thoroughly washed and drained), ginger and garlic paste, and fry for 6–8 minutes till the chicken turns light golden in colour and its surface is sealed. Add red chilli, coriander and turmeric powder and chopped tomatoes. Stir well and cook for 6–8 minutes till the tomatoes are mashed and have mixed well with the chicken.

Next add the green chilli and 1 cup of chopped green coriander. Cook till the mixture starts leaving the oil. If it sticks to the bottom, 1 or 2 tbsp water can be added to prevent the burning of the spices. Cook for 7–8 minutes to achieve this stage. Add salt and 1 cup water, stir well, cover and cook till the chicken is soft and tender.

When cooked, remove lid, sprinkle garam masala powder and remaining coriander, cover and leave it for 3–4 minutes. Mix thoroughly before transferring to a serving dish.

Serve with peas pulao or chapattis.

shakkar ka murg
caramelised chicken
Maharashtra

Preparation time	40 minutes
Cooking time	30–55 minutes
Serves	4–6

Refined oil	5–6 tbsp
Cinnamon	1" stick
Cloves	8–10
Black peppercorn	8–10
Sesame seeds	1½ tsp
Coriander seeds	1 tsp
Cumin seeds	½ tsp
Onions (sliced)	4 (medium)
Tomato (chopped)	2 (medium)
Sugar	1 tbsp
Chicken (cut into 12 pieces)	1 (900 gm–1kg)
Ginger–garlic paste	1½ tbsp
Mint (fresh chopped)	2 tbsp
Turmeric powder	1 tsp
Chilli powder	2 tsp
Garam masala	1 tsp
Curd	1 cup
Salt	To taste (2 tsp)
Green coriander (chopped)	2 tbsp

Heat 2 tbsp oil. Fry cinnamon, cloves, peppercorn, and sesame, coriander, and cumin seeds.

Add sliced onions and brown them. Cool, then add chopped tomatoes with the onion and make a fine paste in a blender.

Now heat a heavy base saucepan or pressure cooker, add sugar and heat till it gets caramelised. The sugar will melt and turn a golden brown colour. Next, add the remaining oil and chicken and fry till it is golden brown. Add ginger-garlic paste and chopped mint, and fry for 4–5 minutes.

Now put in turmeric powder, chilli powder and garam masala powder plus well beaten curd in the chicken. Cook for 2–3 minutes, add the onion paste and salt and mix well. Add water to the desired consistency and cook for 20 minutes (less for pressure cooker) until the chicken is tender and the sauce is smooth.

Transfer to a serving dish. Sprinkle green coriander and serve hot with pulao and fried potatoes.

safed murg
sesame chicken

Maharashtra

Preparation time	15–20 minutes
Cooking time	25 minutes
Serves	4

Refined vegetable oil	3 tbsp
Chicken (deboned and cut into 2" pieces)	1
Green cardamom	4
Cloves	6
Sesame seeds	1 tbsp
Cinnamon	2" stick
Onion (chopped)	2 (medium)
Ginger paste	1 tsp
Garlic paste	¾ tsp
Green chilli (chopped)	2
Salt	To taste (1 tsp)
White pepper powder	½ tsp
Coconut milk	1½ cup
Fresh coriander leaves (chopped)	1 tbsp

Heat the vegetable oil in a thick bottomed pan. Fry the chicken pieces, a few at a time, for approximately 15 minutes till they are golden in colour. Remove and set aside. Now add cardamom, cloves, sesame seeds and cinnamon in the fat and fry for 5 minutes.

Add the chopped onion. Reduce heat and stirring continuously, fry the onions till they are transparent and soft.

Next, add ginger–garlic paste and cook for 5–7 minutes.

Transfer the chicken pieces into the pan and fry for 5–7 minutes.

Add salt, white pepper and the coconut milk. Cook till the chicken is tender and the sauce has thickened.

Sprinkle green coriander and simmer for 3–4 minutes. Serve hot.

hariyali murg
fresh herb chicken curry
Madhya Pradesh

Preparation time	15 minutes
Cooking time	45 minutes
Serves	4

Vegetable oil	3 tbsp
Bay leaf	2
Cumin seeds	1 tsp
Fenugreek seeds	½ tsp
Red chilli (dry)	3 (medium)
Chicken (cut into 12 pieces)	1 (1–1.2 kg)
Spring onion (cut into 1")	24
Ginger (fresh) (cut into thin julienne)	2"
Garlic (chopped)	3 cloves
Fresh mint leaves (roughly chopped)	8–10
Green coriander	3 tbsp
Green chilli (finely chopped)	2
Salt	To taste (2 tsp)
Water	1 cup
Garam masala	1 tsp

Heat the oil in a heavy base pan or in a pressure cooker. Add the bay leaf, cumin seeds, fenugreek seeds and red chilli.

When the seeds crackle add the chicken pieces and gently stir and fry them until the surface of the chicken is sealed to a golden brown colour.

Now add the remaining ingredients except water and cook for 10 minutes.

When the mixture is well mixed, add the water and cover the pan or pressure cooker. Cook for 30 minutes until the chicken is very tender. (Pressure cooker will take less time).

Mix the chicken and sauce well before removing from the fire. If needed, 1 tsp garam masala powder can be sprinkled before serving.

makai murg
chicken with sweet corn

Rajasthan

Preparation time	25 minutes
Cooking time	35–40 minutes
Serves	4

Chicken	1 (900 gms– 1 kg)
Refined oil	3 tbsp
Green cardamom	4
Cloves	4
Cinnamon	2" stick
Bay leaf	1
Mace	2 blades
Onion (chopped)	3 (medium)
Ginger paste	1 tsp
Garlic paste	1 tsp
Green chilli (chopped)	3–4
Chilli powder	1½ tsp
Turmeric powder	1 tsp
Coriander powder	2 tbsp
Yoghurt/Curd	1 cup
Sweet corn kernels (preferably fresh)	1 cup
Salt	To taste (1½ tsp)
Water	1½ cup
Green coriander (chopped)	2 tbsp

Clean, de-skin and cut the chicken into 16 pieces. Wash, pat dry and keep aside.

Heat the refined oil in a sauce pan. Lightly fry cardamom, cloves, cinnamon, bay leaf and mace for 2 minutes. Add chopped onion and chicken pieces. Cook for 8–10 minutes until it is golden brown in colour and extra moisture has dried up.

Add ginger, garlic paste, green chilli, chilli powder, turmeric powder and coriander powder. Cook for 5–7 minutes. When the spices have blended well with chicken add well beaten yoghurt. Cook until the oil separates. Put in the fresh sweet corn kernels, salt and enough water just to cover the chicken.

Simmer for 10–15 minutes till the chicken and corn kernels are tender and sauce is thickened. Sprinkle chopped green coriander and mix well. Serve with chapattis.

Note:
The cooking time will be less if using pressure cooker. If using canned sweet corn, add it a few minutes before the end of cooking.

chicken xacutti

Goa

Preparation time	30 minutes
Cooking time	40 minutes
Serves	4–6

Chicken	1 (1–1.2 kg)
Coriander seeds	½ tsp
Cumin seeds	½ tsp
Fenugreek seeds	1 tsp
Black peppercorn	½ tsp
Peanut (skin removed)	2 tsp
Red chilli (dry)	6–8
Coconut (grated)	½ cup
Cloves	5
Green cardamom	1 tsp
Cinnamon	1" stick
Turmeric powder	1 tsp
Water	3–4 cups
Refined oil	4 tbsp
Salt	To taste
Lemon juice	1 lemon

Clean and cut the chicken into 16 pieces, wash, drain and keep aside.

Heat a frying pan, dry roast the coriander seeds, cumin seeds, fenugreek seeds, black peppercorn, peanuts, dry red chilli and coconut for 2–3 minutes or until light brown in colour. Cool, add cloves, cardamom, cinnamon and turmeric powder. Put in a blender with 3–4 tbs of water and blend to a smooth paste.

Heat refined oil in a saucepan. Put the ground paste and chicken pieces and stir well and fry on low fire until brown in colour adding little water from time to time to prevent sticking at the bottom. Add enough water to cover the chicken pieces. Add salt, mix well, cover and simmer for 15 to18 minutes. Cook till the chicken is tender. Sprinkle lemon juice and mix before serving.

Serve hot with rice.

badami murg
almond chicken

Andhra Pradesh

Preparation time	20 minutes
Cooking time	40–45 minutes
Serves	4–6

Cashewnuts (broken)	1 tbsp
Green cardamom	8–10
Mace	½ tsp
Poppy seeds	2 tsp
Red chilli (dry)	2
Refined vegetable oil	4–5 tbsp
Chicken (cut into 8–12 pieces)	1 (1–1.1 kg)
Onion (blended to puree, add 2 tbsp water if needed)	3 (medium)
Curd/Yoghurt	1 cup
Salt	To taste (2 tsp)
Water	¾ cup
Almond (blanched and skinned)	12–15 pieces
Cream (optional)	2 tbsp

Put cashewnuts, green cardamom, mace, poppy seeds and dry red chilli in a blender with 3 tbsp water and make a smooth paste. If required add more water.

Heat the vegetable oil in a shallow heavy pan. Put in the chicken pieces and fry for 8–10 minutes or until golden brown.

Add the onion puree, cashewnuts, and poppy seeds paste and fry for 4–5 minutes on a slow fire, stirring constantly.

Now add the curd (stirred well) slowly. Add salt, remaining water and the cream, and cover with a lid.

Cook till the chicken is tender. Transfer to a serving dish and garnish with lightly fried almond slices.

I prefer to add few sliced pistachio nuts (soaked in water) on top as they lend a good colour.

murg khada masala
chicken with whole spices
Rajasthan

Preparation time	25 minutes
Cooking time	45 minutes
Serves	4

Mustard oil	4 tbsp
Cumin seeds	1 tsp
Coriander seeds	2 tsp
Black peppercorn	8–10
Cloves	6
Cinnamon	2" stick
Bay leaf	2
Onion (chopped)	3 (medium)
Chicken	1 (1–1.2 kg)
(cut into 8 pieces)	
Ginger (thinly sliced)	1"
Garlic	1 tsp
(peeled and chopped)	
Turmeric powder	1 tsp
Chilli powder	1 tsp
Tomato (chopped)	3–4 (medium)
Salt	To taste (2 tsp)
Water	2 cups
Green coriander	1 tbsp
(chopped)	

Heat the oil in a pan. Add the whole spices and fry for 5 minutes.

Now add the chopped onion and fry till it is golden brown. If necessary, add a few spoons of water to prevent the mixture from sticking to the bottom of the pan.

Next, add the chicken pieces, along with ginger, garlic, turmeric powder and chilli powder. Fry the chicken for at least 25 minutes or till the chicken pieces are well browned.

Add chopped tomatoes and salt and stir for another 5–7 minutes. Pour water and bring to boil. Cook for 10 minutes.

Now reduce heat and simmer for 30 minutes until the chicken is tender and the sauce has thickened. Sprinkle with chopped green coriander.

murg keema hari mirch ka
mince chicken with green chilli
Madhya Pradesh

Preparation time	35 minutes
Cooking time	35–40 minutes
Serves	6

Yoghurt/Curd	½ cup
Ginger (sliced)	1″
Turmeric powder	1 tsp
Chicken mince	900 gms–1 kg
Green chilli	8–10
Ghee/Refined oil	¼ cup
Onion (thinly sliced)	2 (medium)
Cumin seeds	¾ tsp
Garlic (peeled)	4 cloves
Water	3 cups
Salt	To taste (2 tsp)
Lemon juice	1 lemon
Green coriander (chopped)	2 tbsp

Mix yoghurt, ginger and turmeric powder with minced chicken and set aside. De-seed the green chillies, slitting half lengthwise, cut into ½″ long pieces. Keep aside.

Heat ghee/refined oil in a sauce pan. Add sliced onion and fry till the onions are soft. Put the cumin seeds and garlic cloves, and fry for 1–2 minutes. Add the minced meat, stir well and cook for 10–12 minutes.
Add water and salt and cook uncovered for 10 minutes. Then add the green chillies. Cook uncovered till the water dries up and the chicken is cooked. Mix lemon juice and chopped green coriander. Cover and keep aside.

Serve with paratha or roomali roti.

meat

meat

know your ingredients

Black Cardamom (Badi Ilaichi)

These are larger in size and more coarse in texture and taste than the green cardamoms. Often used in meat, poultry, and rice dishes and in the making of garam masala. Bitter in taste with a very strong flavour, they should not be eaten raw.

Mace (Javetri)

Among the most beautiful spices are mace and nutmeg. Small amounts of mace are used in both Hyderabadi and Kashmiri cooking, usually in non-vegetarian food. It is also added to the very rich garam masala from Hyderabad.

Garlic (Lasun)

Garlic has a pungent flavour and should be used in moderation as a flavouring agent. It is said to have medicinal properties and is good for the blood. Never fry garlic in fat or oil which is too hot as it will burn and develop an unpleasant, acrid flavour.

mutton kolhapuri
spicy lamb from kolhapur

Maharashtra

Preparation time	30 minutes
Cooking time	45 minutes
Serves	4–6

Lamb/Mutton (2" cubed)	150 gm
Ginger–garlic paste	1½ tbsp
Cloves	8–10
Black peppercorn	8–10
Green cardamom	4
Mustard seeds (brown)	½ tsp
Poppy seeds	2 tsp
Red chilli (dry)	6–8
Coriander seeds	1½ tsp
Aniseed	1½ tsp
Coconut (grated)	½ cup
Refined oil	¾ cup
Onion (sliced)	4 (medium)
Tomato (chopped)	4 (medium)
Potato (optional, cut into quarters)	3–4
Salt	To taste (2 tsp)
Water	2 cups
Green coriander (chopped)	½ cup

Marinate the meat in ginger and garlic paste. Keep aside.

In the meantime dry-roast cloves, peppercorn, poppy seeds, mustard seeds, green coriander, dry red chilli, coriander seeds, aniseed and grated coconut to a light brown colour in a pan and set aside, to cool.

Heat 2–3 tbsp oil in a big saucepan, add the sliced onion, brown and remove from fire, and cool.

Mix the roasted spices and tomatoes with the brown onion and make a fine paste. Reserve.

In the same pan add the remaining oil and heat. Add the meat and fry to seal the surface and till brown in colour.

Add the potatoes and fry for 4–5 minutes, then add the onion and spice paste and mix well. Add salt and water to get the required gravy consistency. Cover and cook for 30–35 minutes (less time in case of pressure cooker) till the meat is tender and sauce has thickened.

Transfer to a serving dish, decorate with sprinkling chopped coriander on top. Serve with chapattis or boiled rice.

rogan josh
spicy lamb curry
Jammu & Kashmir

Preparation time	30 minutes
Cooking time	45 minutes
Serves	6–8

Mustard oil	4 tbsp
Onion (thinly sliced)	3 (large)
Lamb (preferably the leg portion, cut into 1½" to 2" pieces)	1 kg
Curd/Yoghurt	2 cups
Red chilli powder	2 tsp
Salt	2 tsp
Aniseed powder	2 tbsp
Asafoetida	½ tsp
Cloves	6
Ginger paste	2 tsp
Garlic paste	1 tsp
Cinnamon powder	½ tsp
Black cardamom (seeds crushed)	6
Fresh green coriander (chopped)	2–3 sprigs

Note:

The important ingredient of Rogan josh is 'Ratan jote', a dried petal from the Kashmir valley. If available, add a few (approximately 2 gm) in hot water before you start cooking. It gives a rich red colour.

Heat the mustard oil to smoking point in a large heavy base saucepan. Add the sliced onion and fry till golden brown.

Add the meat and fry it for 4–5 minutes. Reduce the heat, add curd (stirred well) and cook on medium heat. Stirring constantly, fry the mixture until the oil begins to separate. Now add the chilli powder, salt, aniseed powder, asafoetida, cloves, ginger, and garlic paste. Mix all the ingredients well. Cover with a lid (tight filling), reduce the heat and simmer gently for approximately 25 minutes to half an hour till the meat is tender and the sauce has thickened.

Add the ground cinnamon and ground black cardamom. Stir well to mix the ingredients. Stirring frequently, cook for another 5 minutes. When the meat is well cooked and the sauce has thickened, add the green cardamom powder and remove from heat.

Sprinkle chopped green coriander and serve hot. This goes well with chapattis or peas pulao.

sag gosht
spinach lamb
Punjab

Preparation time	30 minutes
Cooking time	45 minutes
Serves	6–8

Lamb (cut into small pieces)	1 kg
Curd/Yoghurt	1 cup
Ginger paste	2 tsp
Garlic paste	2 tsp
Cinnamon	2" stick
Bay leaf	2
Green cardamom	6
Black peppercorn	10–12
Fenugreek seeds	½ tsp
Cloves	8
Cumin seeds	1 tsp
Chilli powder	1 tsp
Coriander powder	2 tsp
Garam masala	1 tsp
Salt	To taste (2 tsp)
Spinach (fresh)	500 gm
Ghee/Vegetable oil	4 tbsp
Onion (thinly sliced)	3 (medium)
Ginger (Julienne)	2 tsp
Cream (optional)	As required

Wash, dry and put the meat in a bowl. Add curd to the meat and mix well.

Now add ginger–garlic paste and mix well. Add the whole and ground spices including the salt, mix well, cover and leave to marinate.

Wash and chop the fresh spinach, heat the ghee/vegetable oil in a thick-bottomed pan or in a pressure cooker, add the sliced onion and fry till golden brown.

Put the marinated meat in the pan, cook over low heat for about 30 minutes until all the moisture has evaporated and the meat is tender.

Add the chopped spinach, mix well and cook for 6–8 minutes until the ghee starts to separate a little.

Transfer the meat to a serving dish, garnish with julienne of ginger and dots of fresh cream (optional).

mutton ka soola
lamb kabab
Rajasthan

Preparation time	20–25 minutes+ marination time
Cooking time	15–20 minutes
Serves	4

Ginger–garlic paste	1 tbsp
Salt	To taste (¾ tsp)
Mutton leg (deboned)	500 gm (cut into 1"cube)
Curd/Yoghurt (hung in muslin cloth for 30 minutes)	1 cup
Red chilli powder	1 tsp
Lemon juice	½ lemon
Garam masala	1 tbsp
Mustard oil	2 tbsp

Onion Salad

Onion (sliced)	2 (medium)
Chaat masala	1 tsp
Green coriander (chopped)	2 tbsp

Rub the ginger–garlic paste and salt in the mutton cubes and leave it to rest for 1 hour.

Make the onion salad by sprinkling chaat masala and chopped green coriander on the onion. Keep it in the refrigerator.

In the meantime, light a charcoal grill or pre heat an oven to 300° C. Put the mutton cubes in a bowl. Add the curd, red chilli powder, lemon juice, garam masala powder and mustard oil. Mix thoroughly and keep for 10–15 minutes.

Now thread the mutton cubes on skewers and grill or broil, brushing them with oil from time to time. Rotate the skewer periodically till the mutton is tender and evenly golden brown in colour.

Scatter the onion salad on a serving plate and arrange the salad in the centre. If desired, lemon juice can be sprinkled just before serving.

papdi gosht
lamb with broad beans
Maharashtra

Preparation time	15–20 minutes
Cooking time	50 minutes–1 hr
Serves	4–6

Refined oil	5 tbsp
Onions (chopped)	4 (medium)
Curry leaves	12–15
Lamb/Mutton (cut into 2" pieces)	750 gm
Ginger–garlic paste	1½ tbsp
Coriander powder	2 tsp
Cumin powder	1½ tsp
Red chilli powder	1½ tsp
Turmeric powder	1 tsp
Garam masala	1 tsp
Water	1½ cup
Potato (peeled and 2" diced)	2 (medium)
Salt	To taste (2 tsp)
Broad beans (strings removed, cut into 2" size)	300 gm
Green coriander (chopped)	½ cup

Heat oil and fry the onions for 3–4 minutes. Add the curry leaves and meat pieces and fry for a few minutes. Cover and cook on slow fire for 15–20 minutes.

Now add ginger–garlic paste, coriander, cumin, red chilli and turmeric powder and fry for 4–5 minutes.

Add 1 cup of water and cook till the meat is nearly done. Then put in potatoes and salt and cook for 5 minutes.

Remove the lid and add beans. Cook till the meat and vegetables are tender. Water can be added, if required. When the meat is cooked, mix it well and adjust the seasoning.

Transfer to a serving dish. Sprinkle chopped green coriander on top. Serve with rice or chapattis.

Best of India

karela gosht
lamb with bitter gourd

Uttar Pradesh

Preparation time	25 minutes
Cooking time	45–50 minutes
Serves	4–6

Bitter gourd	4 (5–6" long)
Salt	To taste (1½ tsp)
Lamb/Mutton (deboned, cut into 1½" dice)	500 gm
Ginger–garlic paste	2 tbsp
Curd/Yoghurt	½ cup
Chilli powder	1 tsp
Turmeric powder	1 tsp
Cumin powder	2 tsp
Coriander powder	1 tbsp
Refined oil	4 tbsp
Onion seeds	1 tsp
Whole fenugreek seeds	1 tsp
Whole mustard seeds (brown)	1 tsp
Water	2½ cups
Garam masala	½ tsp

Wash the bitter gourd, scrape the sides and cut into slices. Dust a pinch of salt on the slices and set aside. Clean and wash the meat. In a medium sized bowl, place the meat and mix well with the ginger–garlic paste, curd, chilli powder, turmeric powder, cumin and coriander powder, and leave it to marinate.

Heat refined oil in a heavy base saucepan or pressure cooker. Add the whole spices in the oil and fry for 3–4 minutes until the spices crackle.

Now add the drained and wiped bitter gourd, fry for 5–7 minutes till the bitter gourd turns pale yellow. Add the marinated meat and fry it till it turns golden brown in colour and the mixture starts leaving the oil. While frying the meat, continuous stirring should be done so that the masala does not stick to the pan.

Add water and cook for 25–30 minutes on low fire, covering the pan, until the meat is tender and the gravy has thickened.

Sprinkle garam masala powder and close the lid. Leave it for 3-4 minutes. Remove from the fire, transfer to a serving dish, and sprinkle chopped green coriander on top before serving. Serve with pulao or paratha.

chukander gosht
lamb/mutton with beetroot
Uttar Pradesh

Preparation time	15 minutes
Cooking time	45–50 minutes
Serves	4

Refined oil	4 tbsp
Lamb/Mutton (deboned and cut to 1½" dice)	500 gm
Beetroot (peeled and chopped)	500 gm
Ginger–garlic paste	1½ tbsp
Turmeric powder	½ tsp
Red chilli powder	1 tsp
Water	2½ cup
Salt	To taste (1½ tsp)
Green coriander (chopped)	1 tbsp

Heat the refined oil in a saucepan. Add the mutton and fry for 2–3 minutes, till the surface of the meat gets sealed and it is light brown in colour.

Add the beetroot and ginger–garlic paste and fry for 5–7 minutes until the beetroot becomes soft and pulpy.

Put the turmeric and chilli powder into the meat and fry for 3–4 minutes. When the spice and meat are well blended, add the water and salt and bring it to boil. Now lower the heat and simmer for 25–30 minutes until the meat is tender and the sauce/gravy has thickened.

Transfer to a serving dish and sprinkle with chopped green coriander before serving. Serve with naan, parathas, or chapattis.

lucknawi korma
lamb curry from lucknow
Uttar Pradesh

Preparation time	20 minutes
Cooking time	40–45 minutes
Serves	4

Lamb (boneless)	500 gm
Onion (chopped)	4 (medium)
Garlic	4 cloves
Ginger	2"
Vegetable oil	3 tbsp
Green cardamom	6
Black cardamom	2
Cinnamon (finely ground)	2" stick
Black peppercorn	8–10
Cloves	4
Salt	To taste (1 tsp)
Coriander powder	2 tsp
Chilli powder	1 tsp
Curd/Yoghurt	5 tsp
Fresh coriander leaves (chopped)	1 tbsp

Remove excess fat from the meat cut into 1" cubes. Keep one chopped onion aside. Put the remaining onions, garlic, and ginger in a blender and make a smooth paste.

Heat the oil in a pan or pressure cooker add the chopped onion, stirring frequently, and fry to a golden brown colour.

Add the ground spices and salt. Stir for 2 minutes, add the meat and fry it for 8–10 minutes to a rich brown colour or till the oil separates from the meat.

Add the onion paste. Continue stirring for 10 minutes till the mixture is well browned. Add the chilli powder and coriander powder. Stir well, add the curd and fry for 10 minutes.

The masala will begin to stick to the bottom of the pan. This is an indication that the meat has been cooked enough.

Add one cup of water, mix well, cover and simmer till the meat is tender and the sauce has thickened. Sprinkle with chopped coriander and serve hot with parathas.

gosht pasanda
lamb pasanda
Uttar Pradesh

Preparation time	30 minutes
Cooking time	45 minutes
Serves	4

Lamb (cut into 2" pieces)	750 gm
Vegetable oil	4–5 tbsp
Onion (sliced)	4 (medium)
Ginger (finely chopped)	1½" piece
Garlic (finely chopped)	3–4 cloves
Turmeric powder	1 tsp
Chilli powder	¾ tsp
Cumin powder	1 tsp
Coriander powder	2 tsp
Salt	To taste (2 tsp)
Cinnamon	2" stick
Cardamom	4
Bay leaf	2
Tomato (chopped)	4 (medium)
Egg (hard boiled, peeled and coarsely chopped)	2
Green coriander (chopped)	2 tbsp

Trim excess fat from the meat pieces. Heat a pan (or pressure cooker). Add 3 tbsp of oil and put in the meat pieces.

Add ¾ of sliced onion, chopped ginger and garlic, turmeric powder, chilli powder, cumin and coriander powder, and salt and fry for 3–4 minutes. Cover with a lid and cook till the meat is nearly done.

Meanwhile, heat the remaining oil in a pan, add the cinnamon, cardamom and bay leaf, and stir-fry for 1–2 minutes. Add chopped tomatoes and cook for 4–5 minutes until they are reduced to pulp.

Add the tomato mixture to the cooked meat and onions. Stir well to mix all the ingredients. Cover and cook for another 7–8 minutes.

Add the chopped boiled egg and mix well. Check the seasoning. Sprinkle chopped green coriander. Serve hot.

aattirachi
kerala lamb curry
Kerala

Preparation time	25–30 minutes
Cooking time	40–45 minutes
Serves	4

Lamb (mutton with bones)	500–600 gm
Refined oil	3 tbsp
Curry leaves	6–8
Green cardamom (crushed)	4
Black peppercorn	¹/₂ tsp
Water	1 cup
Salt	To taste (1 tsp)
Green coriander (chopped)	2 tbsp

To make paste

Onion (sliced)	2 (medium)
Ginger (chopped)	1 tsp
Garlic (peeled)	4–5 cloves
Tomato (sliced)	2 (medium)
Turmeric powder	³/₄ tsp
Red chilli (dry, broken and soaked)	4
Green chilli (chopped)	3
Mustard seeds (brown)	1 tsp
Black peppercorn	¹/₂ tsp
Coriander seeds	1 tsp

Trim the excess fat from the lamb. Clean and cut into 1¹/₂" cubes. Keep aside.

Put all the ingredients except curry leaves, cardamom, peppercorn, salt and green coriander in a blender and blend to a smooth paste. Set aside.

Heat refined oil in a thick bottom pan. Fry curry leaves, cardamom and peppercorn for 1–2 minutes.

Add the ground paste and mix well with the meat. Cook for 15–18 minutes on low heat. Pour water and add salt. Bring to boil. Cover and simmer for 8–10 minutes until the meat is tender and sauce is thick.

Sprinkle chopped green coriander. Serve hot with plain rice.

pork vindaloo

Preparation time	15 minutes
Cooking time	45 minutes
Serves	4–5

Pork (lean and firm)	500 gm
Salt	To taste (1 tsp)
Water	2 cups
Red chilli (dry)	4
Onion (chopped)	2 (medium)
Cumin seeds	1 tsp
Cloves	4
Black peppercorn	6
Cinnamon	½" stick
Ginger paste	1 tsp
Garlic paste	1 tsp
White vinegar	4 tbsp
Vegetable oil	4 tbsp

Trim excess fat and cut the pork into 1" pieces. Boil the meat in a saucepan with salt and water. Remove the scum and cook till the meat is tender. Take the meat from the fire and set aside. Keep the stock to be used later.

Dry roast all the spices to golden brown and cool. Put the roasted spice and vinegar in a blender to make a smooth paste.

Heat the oil in a thick-bottomed pan. Add the chopped onion and fry for 8–10 minutes until golden in colour. Add the spices, ginger, garlic and vinegar paste and fry for 5–8 minutes.

Next add the pork pieces. Stir well, then add the pork stock. Cover and cook for 15 minutes until the pork is very tender and the sauce is reduced.

Serve hot with plain boiled rice.

nargisi salan
lamb with egg & spinach
Uttar Pradesh

Preparation time	15 minutes
Cooking time	40 minutes
Serves	6–8

Ghee/Vegetable oil	6 tbsp
Onion (thinly sliced)	3 (medium)
Lamb/Mutton (deboned, cut into small cubes)	750 gm
Water	2 cups
Cloves	6–8
Cinnamon	2" stick
Green cardamom	8–10
Black peppercorn	6–8
Ginger	½ " piece
Coriander powder	1 tbsp
Salt	To taste (2 tsp)
Saffron	A few strands
Spinach	500 gm
Eggs (beaten)	2
Brown onion	2 tbsp
Cream (optional)	1 tbsp

Heat 4 tbsp ghee/vegetable oil in a thick-bottomed saucepan or in a pressure cooker. Fry the sliced onion in the ghee till it is golden brown.

Now add the meat pieces and fry for 6–7 minutes. When the surface of the meat is sealed add water and (pressure) cook it till the meat is tender.

In the meantime, make a smooth paste of cloves, cinnamon, cardamom, peppercorn, ginger and coriander powder in a food processor or blender.

Add the spice paste, salt and saffron strands and mix well. Cook for 8–10 minutes. Set aside.

Fry the chopped spinach in the remaining ghee. Next add the beaten eggs and cook for 5 minutes. When cooked, add spinach in the meat mixture and cook for 5 minutes.

Transfer to a serving dish, sprinkle brown onion and cream, if desired. Serve with biryani, rice or parathas.

hare masale ka gosht
lamb with green onion
Bihar

Preparation time	15 minutes
Cooking time	40–45 minutes
Serves	4

Lamb	700 gm
Ghee/Vegetable oil	4 tbsp
Spring onion (cut into 1" pieces)	24 (4 bunches)
Garlic paste	³/₄ tsp
Ginger paste	1 tsp
Bay leaf	2
Red chilli powder	1 tsp
Coriander powder	1 tsp
Tomato (chopped)	4–5 (medium)
Green coriander (chopped)	6 sprigs
Salt	To taste (1 tsp)
Garam masala	¹/₂ tsp

Trim excess fat from the meat. Cut into 1½" to 2" pieces, wash and dry.

Heat ghee/vegetable oil in a pan or pressure cooker. Add the meat and stir fry for 8–10 minutes till it is golden brown.

Add all the ingredients except green coriander and garam masala. Stir for 10–12 minutes on a slow fire.

Add one cup of water. Cover with a tight lid and cook till the meat is tender.

Sprinkle garam masala powder and chopped green coriander before removing from the fire. Serve with chapattis or parathas.

mutton shahidi
lamb stew
Uttar Pradesh

Preparation time	20–25 minutes
Cooking time	45–55 minutes
Serve	4–6

Refined oil	3–4 tbsp
Bay leaf	3
Cardamom (black)	2
Black pepper	½ tsp
Onion (thinly sliced)	3 (medium)
Ginger–garlic paste	2 tbsp
Cardamom (green)	6
Mace	2 strands
Cloves	6–8
Mutton (deboned) (cut into 1½" pieces)	500 gm
Water	4 cups
Curd/Yoghurt	½ cup
Salt	To taste (1½ tsp)
Yellow chilli powder	1 tsp

Heat the refined oil in a thick bottomed saucepan. Add bay leaf, black cardamom and black peppercorn. Fry for 1–2 minutes.

Add the sliced onion and fry till the onions are transparent and soft. Now add the ginger-garlic paste and fry for another 4–5 minutes until the onions are golden brown in colour. Put green cardamom, mace, cloves and stir-fry for 1–2 minutes.

Next add the mutton pieces and fry for 5–7 minutes until the meat turns golden in colour. Add ½ cup water and stir well. Cover and let the meat simmer on low fire for 15–20 minutes till it is soft and almost cooked.

Add curd and mix thoroughly. Raise the heat and fry for 4–5 minutes till the curd separates the fat. Add salt, and yellow chilli powder and stir a little. Add the remaining water and bring it to boil. Lower the heat, cover and let it simmer for another 5–7 minutes until the meat is very tender and the sauce has blended well.

Transfer to a serving dish and serve hot. Serve with roomali roti, naan or tawa paratha.

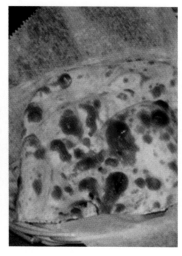

rice and
_____
bread

know your ingredients

Cinnamon (Dalchini)

Cinnamon is the bark of a tree grown in the tropical forests of Sri Lanka, south India and other Asian countries. True cinnamon is recognised by the beautiful quills sold in most supermarkets. It has a very strong flavour. A very small piece is enough to flavour a dish. Cinnamon is also a 'warm' spice and is an essential ingredient in garam masala.

Cloves (Lavang)

Cloves are dried flower buds from evergreen trees which grow in profusion in the monsoon forests all along the southern coast of India. The good ones are well formed, plump and oily. The essential oil extracted from cloves provides relief from toothaches, but if this is not available, chewing one or two cloves will do. They are also used in pickles as a preservative and are an essential ingredient in garam masala. Used in meat, poultry, fish and rice preparations.

Black Cumin (Shahi Jeera)

This is a very aromatic spice, to be used in small quantities. It is most commonly used in rich meat and poultry dishes and is an essential ingredient for making the rich biryanis.

thakkali saadham
tomato rice
Tamil Nadu

Preparation time	10 minutes
Cooking time	20 minutes
Serves	4–6

Basmati rice	1½ cup (300 gm)
Ghee/Vegetable oil	2 tbsp
Mustard seeds	¾ tsp
Curry leaves	14–16
Red chilli (dry)	2 (medium)
Tomato (pureed in a blender)	4 (medium)
Salt	To taste (1–1½ tsp)
Coconut milk (optional)	1 cup
Water	1½ cup
Green coriander (chopped)	1 tbsp

Wash the rice and soak in plenty of cold water for 20 minutes, drain and set aside. Heat the ghee/vegetable oil in a heavy-bottomed saucepan or pressure cooker. Add mustard seeds, curry leaves and the dry red chilli.

When it starts popping add the tomato and salt. Cook for 4–5 minutes. Now add the coconut milk and stir for 2 minutes. Next, add the drained rice and stir-fry it for a few minutes. Level the rice with a flat spoon and pour water to cover the rice by 1″ (approximately 2-finger level). Cover, reduce heat, and cook for 15–18 minutes. If using a pressure cooker follow the company's instructions. Cook the rice until all the water has evaporated and the rice is tender.

Leave it to rest for 2 minutes. Remove lid and let the steam out by using a rice ladle or fork. Serve hot as part of the main meal. Sprinkle chopped coriander before serving.

jeera pulao
cumin rice

Delhi

Preparation time	10 minutes
Cooking time	20–25 minutes
Serves	4–6

Basmati rice	1½ cup
Ghee/Vegetable oil	1 tbsp
Bay leaf	2
Cumin seeds	1 tsp
Onion (sliced) (optional)	1 (medium)
Salt	To taste (1 tsp)
Water	As required

Wash and soak the rice in cold water for approximately 15–20 minutes. Drain thoroughly in a sieve and let it stand for some time.

Heat the ghee/vegetable oil in a heavy base saucepan or pressure cooker. Add the bay leaves and cumin seeds. As soon as they splutter add the sliced onion and fry for 3–4 minutes or until transparent and soft.

Add the drained rice and salt and fry for 2 minutes. Level off the rice in the pan, add enough water to cover the rice by 2 finger 1" level. Cover the pan or pressure cooker and cook for 18–20 minutes on a low fire. In case of pressure cooker follow the particular company's instructions.

Leave the rice to rest for a few minutes. Now open the lid and fluff the rice with a fork or rice spoon.

Transfer to a serving dish. Serve hot. It is a very common accompaniment to many main dishes.

navrattan pulao
mixed vegetable rice
Delhi

Preparation time	10–15 minutes
Cooking time	35–40 minutes
Serves	4–6

Basmati rice	1½ cup
Ghee	2 tbsp
Royal cumin	1 tsp
Bay leaf	2
Onion (sliced)	1 (medium)
Cinnamon	2" stick
Green cardamom	4–6
Black peppercorn	8–10
Cauliflower (1" florets)	6–8
Carrots (cut into ½" cube)	1 (medium)
Green peas	2 tbsp
Beans (½"diced)	2 tbsp
Cottage cheese (cut into ½"cubes)	2 tbsp
Turmeric powder	½ tsp
Chilli powder	1 tsp
Salt	To taste
Sugar	1 tsp
Water	As required

Clean, wash and soak the rice in cold water for 15–20 minutes. Drain the rice and let it stand for 3–4 minutes.

Heat the ghee in a heavy base saucepan or pressure cooker. Add royal cumin and bay leaves and fry for 2 minutes. Next, add the onion and fry to a golden colour.

Put in all the whole spices and fry for 2–3 minutes. Add the vegetables, cottage cheese, turmeric powder and chilli powder and stir-fry for 3–4 minutes. Lower the heat and allow to cook for another 2 minutes.

Add rice, salt and sugar and gently stir well to mix all the ingredients. Add enough water to cover the rice by 1½", lower the heat and cover and cook undisturbed for 16–18 minutes or until the water has evaporated and the grains are separated. If it is cooked in a pressure cooker follow the company's instructions.

Let the rice remain for 3–4 minutes. Fork the rice to the bottom gently to let the steam out. Transfer to a serving dish and serve hot. It may be served with any korma, lentil or raita.

mutton pulao
lamb rice
Uttar Pradesh

Preparation time	20 minutes
Cooking time	40–45 minutes
Serves	4–6

Lamb/Mutton (with bone, cut into 1½" dice)	500 gm
Green cardamom	4
Black peppercorn	6
Cinnamon stick	1" stick
Royal cumin seeds	½ tsp
Bay leaf	1
Red chilli (dry)	2
Salt	To taste (2 tsp)
Water	4½ cups
Basmati rice	2½ cups
Vegetable oil/Ghee	3 tbsp
Onion (finely sliced)	2
Ginger (finely chopped)	1½"
Garlic (chopped)	2 cloves
Chilli powder	1 tsp
Coriander powder	2 tsp

Place the meat, all the whole spices, salt and water in a heavy base saucepan. It can be cooked in a pressure cooker also, which will take lesser time. Cook till the meat is tender.

Strain the meat and reserve the stock. Wash, clean and soak the rice in cold water (for 10–15 minutes), drain and set aside. Heat the vegetable oil/ghee in a heavy base pan. Add the onion and fry for 4–5 minutes. Next add ginger, garlic, chilli powder and coriander powder. Stirring continuously fry for 10–12 minutes till the meat turns golden brown in colour.

Place the drained rice in a saucepan. Add enough reserve stock to cover the rice. Boil for 10 minutes.

When the rice is ¾ cooked and the stock is absorbed, carefully add the rice to the browned meat and mix gently.

Add one cup of remaining stock or water. Cover lightly and cook for 8–10 minutes until the rice is tender.

Fluff the rice with a slicer and transfer it to a serving dish. Serve with a vegetable dish or lentil and yoghurt (curd).

guchchi pulao
mushroom rice
Kashmir

Preparation time	10 minutes
Cooking time	20 minutes
Serves	4–6

Basmati rice	1½ cup
Mushroom (fresh, sliced)	1 cup
Black mushroom (dried)	25 gm
Ghee	3 tbsp
Royal cumin	½ tsp
Kashmiri red chilli (dry)	1
Bay leaf	2
Onion (thinly sliced)	1 (medium)
Cinnamon	1½″ stick
Salt	To taste (1½ tsp)
Fried brown onion	2 tbsp

Wash the rice in cold water and soak it for 15–20 minutes. If using dried mushroom soak in warm water for 15 minutes, drain and cut into ½″ pieces.

Heat a heavy base saucepan or pressure cooker. Put ghee in the pan and heat it to smoking point.

Add cumin, dry red chilli and bay leaves. Stir for a few minutes. Now add the sliced onion and cinnamon stick and fry till the onions are light golden in colour.

Add the mushroom slices and salt, stir-fry for 2 minutes, lower the heat and level the rice with a wooden spoon. Pour enough water to cover the rice by approximately 1″ in level. Cover and cook for about 15–18 minutes (less time if using a pressure cooker) until all the water is absorbed and the rice is tender.

Stop further cooking and let the rice rest for 2–3 minutes. Open the lid gently, slide a slicer to the bottom of the pan and open the rice to let the steam escape. Transfer the hot fluffy rice into a serving dish and sprinkle fried brown onion on it. Serve as accompaniment to a main dish.

thengai saadham
coconut rice
Andhra Pradesh

Preparation time	10 minutes
Cooking time	18–20 minutes
Serves	4–6

Basmati rice	1½ cup
Coconut (fresh, grated)	½ cup
Refined oil	2 tbsp
Mustard seeds	1½ tsp
Curry leaves	12–14
Red chilli (dry)	2
Salt	1 tsp
Coconut milk	½ cup
Water	3 cups (approx.)

Clean and wash the rice in cold, running water. Soak for 10–15 minutes, drain and leave to rest.

Heat a frying pan or iron tawa and dry roast 1 tbsp grated coconut to a golden brown colour. Cook and keep aside for garnishing. Heat the refined oil in a heavy base saucepan or pressure cooker. Add the mustard seeds, curry leaves and the dry red chilli.

When it starts crackling add the grated coconut and stir for a few minutes. Now add the drained rice and salt and stir well for one minute.

Add the coconut milk and gently mix well. Fry for another 2 minutes, then lower the heat. Level the rice with a wooden spoon, pour enough water to cover the rice by 2 finger-measure or 1" approximately. Cover and cook for 15–18 minutes (less in case of pressure cooker) until the moisture is absorbed and rice is tender. Leave it to rest for a while.

Now open the lid and gently slide a slicer to let the steam off from the rice. Transfer to a serving dish and sprinkle roasted grated coconut on top. Serve with mixed vegetable curry or spicy prawn curry.

bhagala bhaath
cold rice with spiced yoghurt
Karnataka

Preparation time	40–45 minutes
Mixing time	15 minutes
Serves	4

Fresh curd (strained)	4 cups
Sugar	2 tbsp
Salt	To taste
Plain boiled rice (soft and separate)	4 cups
Milk	½ cup
Refined oil	1 tbsp
Mustard seeds (brown)	1 tsp
Red chilli (dry)	2–3
Curry leaves	8–10
Cashewnuts (broken)	2 tbsp

In a big bowl beat the curd till smooth, add sugar and salt and mix thoroughly.

Now add the boiled rice and mix very carefully with a wooden spoon or spatula. Rapid mixing may break the rice granules. Add milk and mix well.

Heat one tablespoon of refined oil in a pan. Add the mustard seeds, red chilli (broken into halves) and curry leaves. As it starts crackling, add the broken cashewnuts and fry till golden brown. Cool.

Now mix the fried nuts and spices with the rice and mix thoroughly. Chill this in the refrigerator and serve as main dish with hot lemon pickle.

avadh gosht biryani
lamb biryani
Uttar Pradesh

Preparation time	20 minutes+ soaking time
Cooking time	50–60 minutes
Serves	4

Lamb meat (boneless) (cut into 2" pieces)	500gms
Salt	To taste (2½ tsp)
Cinnamon	2"stick
Black cardamom	2
Green cardamom	4
Basmati rice	2¼ cups
Ghee	2 tbsp
Bay leaf	2
Royal cumin seeds	½ tsp
Onion (chopped)	3 (medium)
Tomato (chopped)	1 (large)
Ginger paste	1 tsp
Garlic paste	1 tsp
Chilli powder	1 tsp
Turmeric powder	½ tsp
Water	5–6 cups
Saffron	A few strands
Rose water/kewra	1 tsp
Brown onion	2 tbsp

Place the meat, 2 tsp salt water, cinnamon, black cardamom, and green cardamom in a heavy based saucepan. Bring it to boil, cover, allow to simmer on low heat until the meat is almost tender.

Strain through a sieve, reserve the stock and meat separately. Clean, wash and soak the rice in cold water for 15 minutes. Drain and set aside.

Heat ghee in a large heavy base pan. Add bay leaf and royal cumin, stir for 1 minute. Now add chopped onion and fry to golden brown.

Add ginger and garlic paste, add tomatoes, chilli powder, turmeric powder, and fry the mixture for 4–5 minutes till the tomatoes are of pulpy consistency.

Add the strained meat along with the whole spices. Fry on high heat for 10 minutes to a deep brown colour. If the meat sticks to the bottom of the pan, add 1–2 tbsp water. Add the balance salt if required.

Add the drained rice to the meat, and fry for a few minutes. Level the rice and meat in the pan. Carefully pour in the meat stock and top it up with enough water (if required) to cover the rice by 1 inch. Cover with a tight-fitting lid and cook on reduced heat for 15–18 minutes.

Remove lid and sprinkle saffron soaked in one 1 tbsp warm water and rose water or kewra.

Replace the lid at once and cook for another 3–4 minutes. Serve the biriyani hot with fried onion on top. Serve with raita and salad.

hydrabadi murg biryani
chicken biryani
Andhra Pradesh

Preparation time	30–35 minutes
Cooking time	55–60 minutes
Serves	4–6

Chicken (cut into 1x12 pieces)	1 (approx.1kg)
Ginger paste	½ tsp
Garlic paste	1 tsp
Green chilli (minced)	2
Ghee	5–6 tbsp
Onion (finely chopped)	3 (medium)
Green cardamom	6
Cloves	6
Cinnamon	2" stick
Mace	1 flower
Peppercorn	6–8
Curd/Yoghurt	1 cup
Water	5 cups
Fresh mint (chopped)	1 tbsp
Green coriander (chopped)	1 tbsp
Salt	To taste (2 tsp)
Basmati rice	2½ cups
Bay leaf	2
Saffron	A few strands

Clean, wash and drain the chicken. Apply ginger paste, garlic paste and minced green chilli thoroughly. Cover and leave to marinate.

Heat the ghee in a heavy base saucepan and fry the onions to a deep brown. Add 4 green cardamoms, 4 cloves and half of the cinnamon stick, mace and peppercorn.

Fry for 2 minutes, then add the curd and marinated chicken and stirring, frequently fry the chicken for 12–15 minutes adding ½ cup water until the chicken is almost tender. Now add chopped mint, coriander and salt and leave it on a low fire for few minutes.

Wash the rice thoroughly. Drain and keep aside.

In another pan boil water with bay leaves, balance cardamom, cinnamon and cloves. Add the washed rice and bring it to boil. Cook for 10 minutes so that it is half cooked. Drain and keep aside. Save the water for cooking biryani.

Empty the pan of chicken but do not rinse it. Place about 2" layers of rice at the bottom of the pan, then a layer of chicken on top. Repeat this process till the chicken and rice has been used up totally. Pour the balance water just to cover the rice.

Dissolve saffron in warm water in a table spoon and sprinkle over the rice. Cover with a tight-fitting lid and allow to cook on a low fire for 12–15 minutes until the chicken and rice are tender, leave it covered for few minutes.

Fluff the rice with a slicer and serve hot. Serve with raita.

ajwain paratha
carom-flavoured paratha
Uttar Pradesh

Preparation time	20 minutes
Cooking time	20 minutes
Makes	8–10

Whole wheat flour	1¼ cup
Salt	1 tsp
Chilli powder	¾ tsp
Carom seeds	2 tsp
Water	1 cup
Ghee/Vegetable oil	3 tbsp/4 tbsp

Take flour, salt, chilli powder and carom seeds in a bowl. Add water gradually and bind the flour into a smooth dough. Knead for a few minutes, cover with a damp cloth, and leave to rest for 10 minutes.

Divide the dough into 8–10 equal portions of smooth ball. Roll out with the help of a rolling pin, one ball at a time, on a flour-dusted surface into a round of 6" diameter. Spread a little melted ghee or refined oil and fold the paratha into a cylindrical roll.

Roll the cylinder shape dough further like a pin wheel. Flatter the pin wheel and roll back again to 6" diameter. Dust a little dry flour to prevent it from sticking.

Heat a heavy base shallow frying pan or griddle. Carefully place the rolled dough on the hot griddle. Allow to cook for 10–20 seconds until the surface becomes opaque.

Turn the paratha over and smear a little ghee/oil on the surface. Cook the underside for a few seconds, then turn over and repeat the process till both surfaces become crisp and golden brown in colour with dark brown spots. Repeat with remaining dough and serve hot with lime/mango pickle and plain curd.

aloo paratha
potato stuffed paratha
Delhi/Punjab

Preparation time	15 minutes+
	15 minutes boiling of potato
Cooking time	20–25 minutes
Makes	10–12

For dough

Whole wheat flour	4½ cups
Salt	To taste (½ tsp)
Water	1½ cup (approx.)

For Potato filling

Potato	3 (medium)
Onion (chopped)	1 (medium)
Ginger (chopped)	1 tbsp
Green chilli (seeded and chopped)	4
Green coriander (chopped)	2 tbsp
Pomegranate seeds	1 tsp
Red chilli powder	1 tsp
Salt	To taste (1 tsp)
Butter	½ cup

Sieve the flour with salt. Make a bay in the sieved flour, pour water in it and start mixing gradually. When totally mixed, knead with the knuckles to a soft, smooth dough. Cover with a damp cloth and leave it to rest for 10–12 minutes.

Boil, cool, peel and mash the potatoes. Mix well all the ingredients in the mashed potatoes, divide into 10–12 equal portions, cover with a moist cloth and keep aside for 5 minutes.

Place the balls one at a time on flour-dusted surface and roll to 4" diameter with a rolling pin. Place a portion of the potato filling in the centre, enfold the filling and seal the edges. Flatter again with the rolling pin to approximately 7–8" diameter.

Place the paratha on a heated griddle or heavy-bottomed frying pan and cook to opaque, turning over both sides. Smear 2 tbsp butter all around and fry till golden brown in colour and crisp in texture. Serve hot with lime/mango pickle and curd.

puris
fried puffed bread
Delhi

Preparation time	12–15 minutes
Cooking time	15–20 minutes
Makes	24–28

Whole wheat flour	2 cups
Refined flour	1½ cup
Salt	½ tsp
Ghee	2 tbsp
Water (lukewarm)	1 cup
Refined oil	To deep fry

Mix both whole wheat and refined flour and salt thoroughly. Rub the ghee in the flour mixture till it gets mixed properly.

Now add the warm water gradually to the flour, mixing continuously. Make a dough and knead it with the knuckles for 5–7 minutes. Let it rest for 15–20 minutes.

Now divide the dough into 24–28 small equal balls. Flatten one at a time, pressing with the palm. Roll on a floured board to a 4″ round disc.

Heat oil in a wok to smoking point. Slide rolled puris one at a time into the hot oil. It will begin to puff up. Turn it upside down with a perforated spoon and fry for 30–40 seconds until the puri is light golden in colour.

Drain thoroughly and place on a kitchen paper. Repeat the process till all the kneaded dough is over. Serve with vegetables or any curry.

khameeri roti
yeast bread
Jammu & Kashmir

Preparation time	15 minutes+ fermenting time 1 hr
Cooking time	15–20 minutes
Makes	6–8

Sugar	1½ tsp
Milk	½ cup
Whole wheat flour	4 cup
Salt	To taste (½ tsp)
Fennel seeds (coarsely ground)	1 tsp
Ghee	1 tbsp
Yeast (softened)	2 tsp

Melt sugar in the milk. Sieve the flour with salt. Mix ground fennel seeds with 1 tbsp ghee, desired salt and yeast. Mix well.

Add the milk and form into a dough. Knead for 5–6 minutes till the dough is soft and smooth. Leave it covered with a wet cloth to ferment for 45 minutes to 1 hour or until the dough becomes twice the size.

Now divide the dough into even-sized portions, about 6–8. Rotate them one at a time between two palms and form a small round ball.

Roll out each ball into 6" round and dry-cook it on a hot griddle, and then put it directly on open fire so that the rotis puff up. Make all the rotis in the same way and serve with melted ghee on top. Usually served with mutton (rogan josh).

tawa paratha
pan-fried parathas
West Bengal

Whole wheat flour	
Refined flour	4 cups
Salt	½ tsp
Cooking soda	1 pinch
(sodium bicarbonate)	
Ghee	1 cup
Water	1½ tbsp

Preparation time	20–30 minute
Cooking time	15–20 minutes
Makes	8–10

Sieve flour with salt and cooking soda in a large basin or bowl. Add 2 tbsp ghee. Rub well with the flour.

Gradually add water and form a dough. Knead the dough for at least 10–12 minutes until pliable and smooth. Let it rest for 10 minutes. Knead again for 3–4 minutes.

Now divide it into 8–10 portions. Roll each portion on a floured board into a 6–7" disc. Brush the flattered dough (disc) with melted ghee.

Roll from one edge to the other. It takes the shape of a thick stick. Hold one end and circle the dough like a Swiss roll. Press with the palm, roll it again, dusting a little flour, to a 7–8" diameter disc. Repeat the process for the rest of the parathas.

Fry the parathas in a frying pan one at a time, gently basting ghee regularly until golden brown and crisp on both sides.
Drain and store in a covered dish. Serve with gram lentil or mutton preparation.

desserts
esserts desserts
desserts

desserts

know your ingredients

Green Cardamom (Chhoti Ilaichi)

Good quality green cardamoms come with a pungent and very aromatic flavour, pale in colour, and firm to the touch. The seeds inside are black or dark brown and slightly sticky with a white membrane surrounding them. Both husk and seeds are used in cooking sweet as well as savoury dishes. Cardamom is a digestive spice and is often chewed after a meal. It also has medicinal properties and helps to alleviate nausea. When brewed with tea and other spices, it helps to clear sore throats and colds.
It is also an essential ingredient of garam masala.

Saffron (Zaffran or Kesar)

The most expensive spice in the world, saffron is a highly aromatic spice and gives a delicate yellow-orange colour to any dish. A pinch is often enough to colour a fair amount of food. Too much saffron will very often ruin a dish. Turmeric must never be used in place of saffron.

Aniseed or Fennel (Saunf)

An aromatic and digestive spice with distinct, elongated seeds that are a pale green or very light brown in colour. Aniseed is most commonly used in the Bengali and Kashmiri-style cooking, either as a whole spice or ground into a fine powder. Taken after a meal, it can aid digestion and brewed in tea, it can cure mild colds.

phirni
rice flour pudding
Andhra Pradesh

Preparation time	8–10 minutes
Cooking time	40 minutes
Serves	4

Milk	4–5 cups
Rice flour (coarse)	½ cup
Sugar	½ cup
Almonds	10 (cut into slivers)
Rose water	2 tsp
Saffron	A few strands
Pistachio (unsalted)	10–12 (cut into slivers)

Bring ¾ of the milk to a boil in a heavy base deep pan. Simmer (uncovered) gently.

Mix rice flour in the remaining milk and add to the simmering milk. Stirring continuously, bring the milk to a boil, then reduce heat and let it simmer for 30–35 minutes or until the mixture is of a thick consistency and free from any lumps.

Add sugar, almonds, rose water and saffron. Stir well. Cook for 3–4 minutes until the sugar is completely dissolved.

Pour the pudding into small individual serving dishes. Decorate with slivered pistachio. Chill before serving.

gajar ka halwa
carrot halwa
Delhi

Preparation time	30 minutes
Cooking time	45 minutes
Serves	8–12

Milk	5 cups
Carrots (washed, peeled and grated)	900 gm (4–5 cups)
Sugar	1¼ cup
Ghee	5–6 tbsp
Green cardamom (powdered)	½ tsp
Sultanas	2 tbsp
Solidified milk (grated)	3 tbsp
Almonds (blanched & skinned)	2 tbsp
Pistachio (slivered)	

Boil the milk in a wok or wide-faced vessel. Add the grated carrots, reduce the heat and cook, stirring regularly. Cook on a slow fire for 25–30 minutes until the carrots are soft and done and most of the milk has evaporated.

Then add sugar and cook for 8–10 minutes by when all the liquid should evaporate. Fry the halwa for 3–4 minutes and add the cardamom powder and sultanas. Mix well. Transfer to a serving dish. Decorate with grated khoya (solidified milk), and slivered nuts. Serve hot as dessert.

chhena payesh
cottage cheese dessert
West Bengal

Preparation time	35 minutes
Cooking time	30 minutes
Serves	4–6

Milk (full cream)	2½ litre
Lemon juice	1 tsp
Water	½ cup
Granulated sugar	¾ cup
Green cardamom	4
Almonds	10
(blanched and slivered)	
Pistachio nuts	8
(soaked and sliced)	

Boil ½ litre of milk in a saucepan. While boiling, stir continuously so that it does not get burnt at the bottom of the pan.
Add 1 tsp lemon juice and take off the fire. Keep for 6–8 minutes. The milk will curdle and lumps of cheese will be formed.
To strain the whey from the cheese, hang the mixture tied in a muslin cloth for about 30 minutes.

In the meantime, make a thick sugar syrup with water and granulated sugar. The consistency should be such that it coats the back of a spoon (like pure honey).
Place the cheese in a large bowl and slowly pour the syrup, a little at a time, mixing gently once in a while. Pour the whole syrup and fold in delicately. Cover and set aside.
In another saucepan boil remaining 1 litre of milk with cardamom pods broken and put in. Reduce the milk to half, cool it to lukewarm temperature.

Now mix the slivered almonds and pistachio nuts in the milk. Keep some nuts for decorating the top.
Add the reduced milk to the cheese gradually stirring continuously. Continue pouring until all the milk is added to the cheese.
Keep portion as per serving dish and decorate on top with slivered nuts. Refrigerate and serve chilled.

malpua
flour fritters in sugar syrup
West Bengal

Preparation time	15–20 minutes
Cooking time	20 minutes
Makes	10–12

Sugar	1½ cup
Water	2 cups
Bay leaf	1
Plain flour	½ cup
Milk (reduced to approx. 2½ cups)	1 litre
Fennel seeds	½ tsp
Black cardamom	3–4
Ghee	To fry fritters

Boil sugar and water with the bay leaf in a saucepan till it forms a medium thick syrup. Keep aside.

Mix together the flour and reduced milk with a whisk so that there are no lumps and the mixture is very smooth. The batter should be of coating consistency.
Add the fennel seeds and cardamom seeds. Let it stand for 10 minutes.

Heat ghee in a frying pan (preferably non-stick pan) for frying of fritters. Drop 2 tbsp batter at a time in the middle of the pan and fry in the simmering ghee. The batter will spread to about 4–5″ diameter round fritters. Fry till the edges are dark brown and crisp.

Remove with a slotted spoon, draining thoroughly and drop it in the prepared sugar syrup. Let it soak in the syrup for 1–2 minutes.

Remove and keep in a platter with a little syrup coated on it. Repeat the process and make about 12 fritters. Serve hot with syrup as dessert.

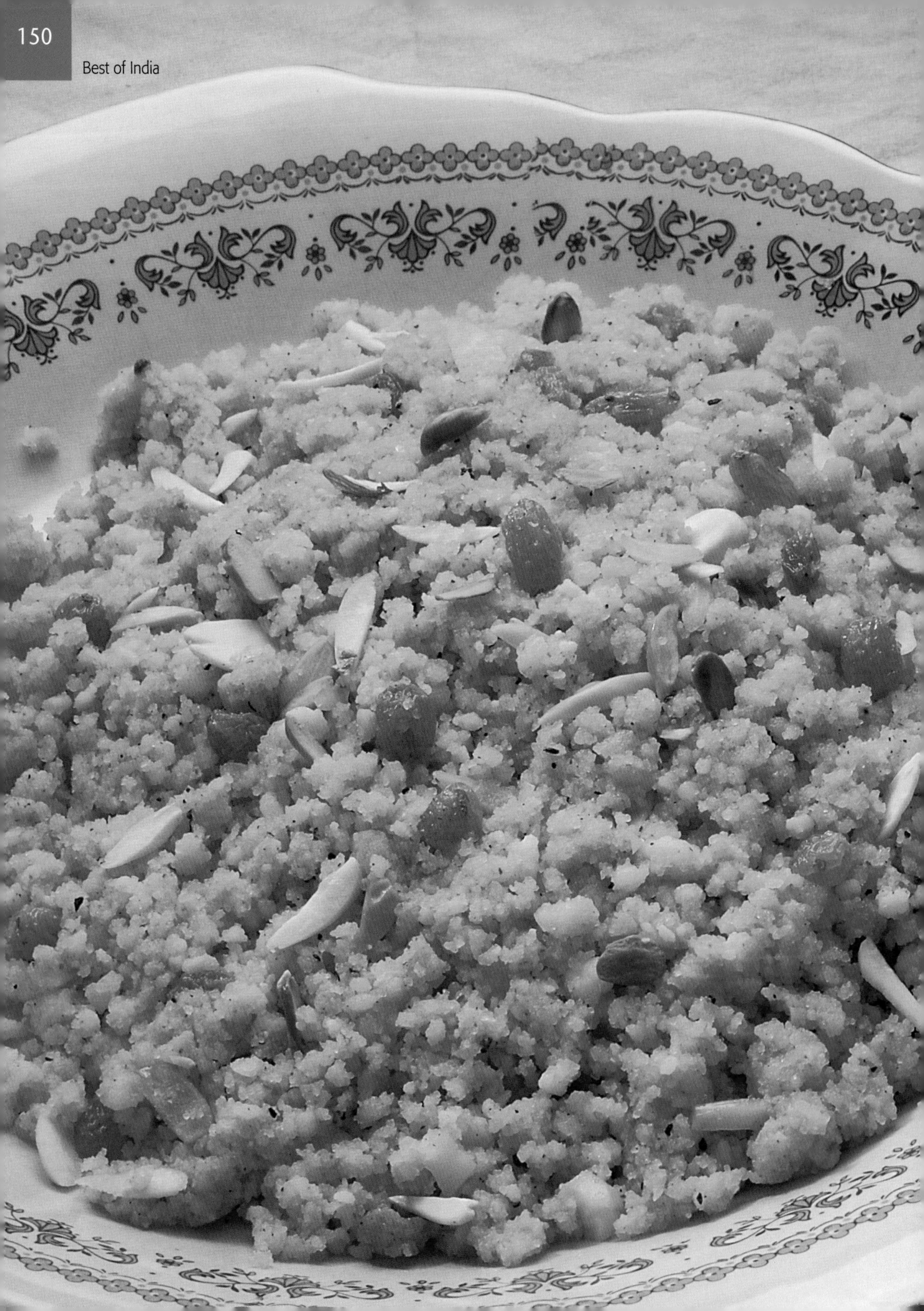

ande ka halwa
aromatic egg halwa
Madhya Pradesh

Preparation time	40 minutes
Cooking time	45 minutes – 1 hr
Serves	6–8

Egg	6
Ghee	½ cup
Semolina	½ cup
Milk	½ cup
Solidified milk (optional)	½ cup
Sugar	½ cup
Green cardamom (powdered seeds)	½ cup
Almond (blanched, peeled and slivered)	10
Pistachio (soaked and sliced)	10–12
Sultanas	1 tbsp
Rose water	1 tbsp

Shell the boiled eggs and separate the white and yolk. Chop the egg whites.

Mash the yolks with the help of a whisk and form into coarse granules. Whisk the egg whites in a blender once or twice just to make into coarse granules. Heat the ghee in a saucepan. Add the semolina and fry till it is golden brown in colour.

Add milk and mix well. Then add egg granules and solidified milk and cook for 10–12 minutes, stirring continuously or until the milk is reduced substantially.

Add sugar and cardamom powder, mix well, and cook for 4–5 minutes.

Next, add almonds, pistachio and sultanas and cook till the mixture thickens. Remove from fire and cool it, stirring from time to time to prevent formation of any layers. Add rose water and set aside, covered.
Serve as dessert. Tastes best when warm.

payasam
bengal gram and milk dessert

Tamil Nadu

Preparation time	20 minutes
Cooking time	45 minutes
Serves	4–6

Water	2 cups (approx.)
Bay leaf	2
Bengal gram (washed and drained)	4 tbsp
Milk	4 cups
Green cardamom (pods cracked)	6
Coconut milk	1 cup
Jaggery	To taste (1/2 cup)
Ghee	3 tbsp
Cashewnuts	3 tbsp
Sultanas	2 tbsp

Put two cups of water in a pan and bring it to a boil. Add the bay leaf, and bengal gram and let it simmer for 8–10 minutes until the lentil is half cooked.

Now put in the milk and green cardamom, cover and let simmer on slow fire for 15 minutes until the lentil is very soft.
Next, add the coconut milk and jaggery and cook, stirring continuously until the mixture thickens to your liking.

Heat ghee in a small frying pan. Add the broken cashewnuts and sultanas, and fry till golden brown.

Pour this over the milk mixture and mix well. Payasam is normally served lukewarm but if desired it can be chilled in which case the consistency would be very thick. Serve as dessert.

badam barfi
almond fudge

Jammu & Kashmir

Preparation time	35 minute+ soaking time
Cooking time	1–1½ hr
Makes	20–24

Almonds (blanched and peeled)	1½ cup
Milk	2 cups
Sugar	1 cup
Water	½ cup
Ghee	1 cup

Soak the almonds overnight in 5–6 cups of water. Skin the almonds and make a smooth paste in a blender or food processor by adding milk.

In a saucepan dissolve the sugar in ½ cup of water and bring it to a boil. Cook the syrup for about 10 minutes or until the syrup is reduced to half.

Add the almond mixture a little at a time, stirring continuously. Care should be taken that the mixture does not stick to the bottom of the pan. Cook for 45 minutes to 1 hour, till the mixture thickens.

Slowly pour the melted ghee into the almond mixture, stirring continuously. The ghee is totally absorbed in the almond paste and the rich almond paste is glossy.

Transfer to a ½" tray or thali and spread the mixture to a thickness of ½". As it starts to set, cut into diamond shapes and leave it to cool. Serve cold as dessert or a sweet snack.

muzaffar anaras ki
sweetened pineapple rice
Uttar Pradesh

Preparation time	45 minutes
Cooking time	1 hr
Serves	6–8

Sugar	2½ cups
Water	¾ cup
Lemon juice	1 lemon
Nutmeg (grated)	¼ tsp
Saffron	12–14 strands
Pineapple essence	4–6 drops
Green cardamom	6–8
Cloves	6
Bay leaf	2
Basmati rice	1¼ cup
Pineapple ring (tinned)	3 (cut into ¼″)
Ghee	2 tbsp

Boil sugar with water and lemon juice and make a thick syrup. Add nutmeg, saffron and pineapple essence. Keep aside.

Heat approximately 6 cups of water in a vessel and add cardamom, cloves and bay leaves and boil for 2–3 minutes.

Now put the cleaned, soaked and drained rice in the water and cook till it is soft. Drain the excess water. Set aside the rice.

Add the cooked rice in the sugar syrup and mix well. Give a boil and remove from fire. Add the pineapple pieces and cover tightly with a lid. Put in dum either in an oven or on a hot tawa for 15–20 minutes.

Sprinkle ghee before serving. It is a popular dessert of Avadh cuisine.

shrikhand
saffron flavoured yoghurt
Maharashtra

Preparation time	25–30 minutes
Chilling time	8 hrs or overnight
Serves	4–6

Fresh curd/Yoghurt	3 cups
Saffron	8–10 strands
Milk	2 tbsp
Sugar (castor)	1 cup
Nutmeg (grated)	2 pinches
Pistachio (soaked and slivered)	10–12

Tie the curd in a muslin cloth and hang for 40–45 minutes. It can also be kept in a sieve over a bowl. By this process the whey will drain away.

Soak the saffron strands in 2 tbsp warm milk for about 10–15 minutes.
Place the drained curd in a glass bowl, add castor sugar, stirring continuously to mix thoroughly.

Add the saffron milk and mix properly. Cream the sweetened curd properly with a wooden spoon and keep portions in individual serving bowls.

Refrigerate for 6–8 hours until it is well set. Sprinkle a little nutmeg powder and pistachio before serving. Though it is a sweet dish, many people like to have it with hot puris.

paal poli
flour puffs in cardamom milk
Tamil Nadu

Plain refined flour	1½ cup
Ghee	3 tbsp
Water	⅓ cup
Milk	4 cups
Sugar	1 cup
Green cardamom (powdered)	½ tsp
Saffron	A few strands

Preparation time	30 minutes
Cooking time	50 minutes
Serves	4

Sieve the flour and rub with ghee against the palms. Slowly add water and make dough. Knead the dough thoroughly to soft and pliable texture. Cover with a moist cloth and set aside.

Boil milk in a saucepan for 30 minutes on low heat stirring constantly until reduced to $1/3^{rd}$. Add sugar, green cardamom and saffron, boil for another 4–5 minutes till the sugar is well dissolved. Remove from fire and set aside. Stir in the milk at regular intervals to prevent any formation of layers.

Heat oil for deep frying in a kadahi or wok. Divide the flour dough into 14 equal portions. Roll each portion with a rolling pin to 4 inches round disc. Slide each disc one at a time into the hot oil. Fry the puffs to light golden colour. Drain from the oil and soak in the reduced milk for 2–3 minutes. Remove and place on a platter. Arrange the puffs in a serving dish and pour little reduced milk on top.

Serve as main dessert after meal.

bhapa doi
steamed yoghurt
West Bengal

Preparation time	20 minutes
Cooking time	35 minutes
Serves	10

Curd/Yoghurt	2½ cups
Pistachio nuts	6–8
Saffron	8–10 strands
Cream	¼ cup
Condensed milk	1 tin
Raisins	2 tbsp

Hang the curd tied in a muslin cloth or put on a sieve for 1 hour to drain the excess water.

Soak the pistachio nuts in cold water for 3–4 hours to get a pure green colour and soft texture. Slice thinly and keep aside.
Soak the saffron strands in the cream.
Take a large glass bowl and mix the hung curd and condensed milk. Whip the milk and curd gently to a smooth and fluffy consistency. Excess whipping of the curd might make the mixture curdle.

Add the saffron cream and half of the sliced pistachio nuts and raisins. Fold in gently to mix all the ingredients thoroughly.
Pour this into an oven-proof dish. Sprinkle remaining nuts on top. Pre heat oven to 400°F. Set the curd dish on a baking tray. Pour boiling water in the tray covering half to three quarter way up the dish. Bake for 25 to 30 minutes or till a tooth-pick inserted in the centre comes out clean. This can also be baked in a microwave oven. Follow the manufacturer's instructions. If using the microwave, curd should not be hung or strained. It can be set in individual containers if you want to serve it separately. Cool, refrigerate and serve chilled as dessert.

potato bibinca
potato coconut cake
Goa

Potato	4 (medium)
Sugar	1½ cup
Water	¾ cup
Plain flour	4 tbsp
Semolina	2 tbsp
Coconut milk (thick)	2 cups
Egg	6
Butter	6 tbsp
Nutmeg (powder)	1 tsp

Preparation time	35 minutes
Cooking time	40–45 minutes
Serves	8–10

Boil the potatoes with the skin and cool. Remove skin, mash and set aside.

Mix sugar with ¾ cup of water and boil over medium heat to make sugar syrup. Cool it. Add flour, semolina and 1 cup of coconut milk and mix well. Fold in the yolks of the eggs one at a time to the milk, beating constantly. Add mashed potatoes and the remaining coconut milk.

Beat the egg whites well and add to the potato mixture. Melt the butter, add the nutmeg powder and pour in the batter. Mix well. Prepare a cake tin. Put the batter and bake in a preheated oven (175°C) for 30–35 minutes.

Cool and serve cutting into slices as per requirement.

basic recipes

Coconut Milk

| Coconut | 1 |
| Water (lukewarm) | 1½ cup |

Break the coconut taking care to reserve the water. Break open the white flesh from the hard shell. Remove the brown skin, grate the white coconut and put in a blender. Add 1 cup lukewarm water (if the coconut water is saved that can be strained and added to give a better flavour). Liquidise to a smooth consistency. Strain the liquid through a fine sieve, pressing with the back of a round spoon. The process is repeated again with the residue and the remaining ½ cup lukewarm water. The milk is refrigerated and used as per recipe.

Curd (Yoghurt)

| Milk | 1 litre |
| Natural curd | 1 tbsp |

Boil milk in a saucepan and cool it. It should be neither too hot nor too cold. The best way to check is to put in a clean finger and feel the temperature. It should be lukewarm. Pour the milk into a warm container, add the natural curd and gently mix it. Then put a lid and cover with towel or warm cloth. Leave it to set for 8 hours without disturbing the container (the timing depends on the climatic temperature). When it is set, refrigerate for 2–3 hours and use as per requirement.

Tamarind Pulp

| Ripe tamarind pods | 100 gm (deseeded) |
| Water | 100 ml (1/2 cup) |

Soak the tamarind in lukewarm water for at least 30 minutes to soften and loosen the pulp. Mash the tamarind and press through a sieve. Discard the residue. Use the pulp as per recipe.

Paneer/Cottage Cheese

| Milk | 5 cups |
| Fresh lemon juice | 4 tsp or 4 tsp vinegar (white) |

Boil the milk in a saucepan stirring continuously. Remove from fire and add 4 tsp fresh lemon juice or white vinegar. Stir a little and keep aside. The milk curdles and the paneer will separate. Let it stand to coagulate for 10–12 minutes. Strain through a muslin cloth. The whey can be saved and used for cooking in place of water or even for cracking the milk to make paneer. For flattening the paneer to 1½" thickness, wrap in muslin cloth and put some weight on it for 2–3 hours. Remove and refrigerate. Cut and use as per requirement.

Ginger–Garlic Paste

Fresh ginger	100 gm
Garlic	100 gm
Water	2–3 tbsp

Remove the skin, wash and roughly chop the ginger. Peel the garlic pods and crush with the back of a spoon or knife. Grind ginger and garlic with water to a fine paste. Keep it in the refrigerator for regular use. It can be stored in the deep freezer in a closed container for 2–3 months. The same procedure can be followed to make ginger and garlic paste separately.

Paanch Foran

Cumin seeds
Nigella
Aniseed
Brown mustard seeds
Fenugreek seeds

Equal quantities of all the spices are mixed together and used as per recipe. This is a specialty spice blend used by the Bengalis of eastern India. The best way is to keep ready mixed spices handy. Literally, in Bengali 'paanch' means 'five' and 'foran' means 'tempering'.

Garam Masala

The literal meaning is warm spice. Various types of garam masalas are used all over India. There have been garam masala mixtures for each region, for vegetarian and non-vegetarian dishes, and individual tastes. The powdered spice generally loses its aroma and its strength due to evaporation of essential oils. It is better to have small quantities ground freshly as per requirement. The mix of garam masala provided here is the basic and can be used uniformly in various dishes. This is in a milder form which does not burn the tongue or make the dish hot.

Cinnamon	4 (1" sticks)
Cloves	2½ tsp
Green cardamon	15–20

In a dry grinder, grind all the spices to a fine powder. Store in an airtight container and use as per recipe.

glossary

English	Hindi
Almond	Badam
Alum	Phitkari
Aniseeds	Saunf
Asafoetida	Hing
Aubergine/Brinjal	Baigan
Bay leaves	Tejpatta
Beetroot	Chukandar
Bengal gram (split)	Chana dal
Bitter gourd	Karela
Black cardamom	Badi illaichi
Black beans	Urad
Broad beans	Sem/Papdi
Buttermilk	Chhas
Brown Mustard seeds	Rai
Cabbage	Band gobhi
Cardamom(green)	Choti illaichi
Carrot	Gajar
Carom seeds	Ajwain
Caraway seeds	Shahi jeera
Cashewnuts	Kaju
Cauliflower	Phool gobhi
Cinnamon	Dalchini
Cloves	Lavang
Coconut	Nariyal
Colocasia	Arbi
Coriander seeds	Dhania
Coriander leaves	Hara dhania
Cottage Cheese	Paneer
Cumin seeds	Jeera
Curry leaves	Meetha neem patta

English	Hindi
Dry apricot	Khubani
Dry fig	Anjeer
Dry plums	Alu bukhara
Fenugreek leaves	Methi
Fenugreek seeds	Methi dana
Fresh corn	Makai
Fresh green gram	Hara chana
Fresh mint leaves	Pudina
Garlic	Lahsun
Ginger	Adrak
Gram flour	Besan
Green chilly	Hari mirch
Green coconut	Hara nariyal
Jackfruit	Kathal
Lentil (red)	Masoor dal
Lemon	Nimboo
Mango powder	Aamchur
Mace	Javitri
Marrow	Doodhi
Millet	Bajra
Jaggery	Gur
Mustard oil	Sarson ka tel
Nigella	Kalonji
Onion	Peyaj
Onion seeds	Kalonji
Okra	Bhindi
Peanuts	Moongphali
Pistachio	Pista
Poppy seeds	Khus khus
Radish	Muli

English	Hindi
Red chilly	Lal mirch
Red pumpkin	Kaddu
Refined flour	Maida
Rice flour	Chawal ka atta
Raisins	Kishmish
Semolina	Suji/Sooji
Sesame seeds	Til
Split green gram	Moong dal
Split black gram	Urad dal
Solidified milk	Khoa/mawa
Tamarind	Imli
Turmeric	Haldi
Turnip	Shalgum
Vermacelli	Sevian
Walnut	Akhrot
Wild fig	Goolar
Whole wheat flour	Atta
Yellow lentils	Arhar dal
Yellow mustard seeds	Sarson

weights and measures

Ounce	Grams
1	28
2	57
3	85
4	113
5	142
6	170
7	198
8	227
9	225
10	284
11	312
12	340
13	369
14	397
15	425
16(1lb)	454

1 gram	=	0.035 ounce
10 grams	=	0.35 ounce
100 grams	=	3.5 ounce
200 grams	=	7.0 ounce

1 tea spoon (tsp)	=	5 g
2 tsp	=	10 g
3 tsp	=	15 g

1 table spoon (tbs)	=	15 g

1/4 cup	4 tbs or 2 oz
1/3 cup	5 tbs + 1tsp
1/2 cup	8 tbs or 4oz
2/3 cup	10 tbs + 2tsp
3/4 cup	12 tbs or 6oz
1 cup	16 tbs or 8oz
1 cup (liquid)	240 ml
16 oz (liquid)	2 cups or 1 pint
2 pints (liquid)	4 cups or 1 quart

Measures for commonly used ingredients in the book

Ingredient	Measure	Weight
Coriander (chopped)	1 cup	60g
	1 tbs	4 g
Green Peas (shelled)	1 cup	160g
Mint (chopped)	1 cup	60 g
	1 tbs	4g
Onions (chopped)	1 cup	170g
Tomatoes (chopped)	1 cup	225g
All lentils (dals)	1 cup	200g
Dry beans	1 cup	200g
Rice	1 cup	200g
Atta (whole wheat flour)	1 cup	120g
Gram flour (besan)	1 cup	150g
Flour (maida)	1 cup	125g
Ghee or vegetable fat	1 cup	200g
	1 tbs	12g
Groundnut oil/refined oil	1 cup	220g
	1 tbs	15ml
Mustard oil	1 cup	220g
	1 tbs	15ml
Milk	1 cup	240ml
Yoghurt	1 cup	225g
Cream	1 cup	250ml
Sugar	1 cup	200g
	1 tbs	12g
Carom seeds (ajwain)	1 tsp	2.5g
	1 tbs	7.5g
Onion seeds (kalonji)	1 tsp	3.5 g
	1 tbs	10g
Coriander seeds (dhania)	1 tsp	2g
	1 tbs	6g
Cumin seeds (jeera)	1 tsp	3g
	1 tbs	9g
Fennel seeds (saunf)	1 tsp	2.5
	1 tbs	7.5
Fenugreek seeds (methi dana)	1 tsp	4.5g
	1 tbs	14g

Dry fenugreek (kasturi methi)	1 tbs	12g
Poppy seeds (khus khus)	1 tsp	3g
	1 tbs	9g
Sesame seeds (til)	1 tsp	3.5g
	1 tbs	10.5g
Powdered spices (all varieties)	1 tsp	5g
Boiled onion paste	1 cup	240g
Garlic paste/ginger paste	$1^3/_4$ tsp	10g
Garlic paste/ginger paste	$2^1/_2$ tsp	15g
	4 tsp	25g
	3 tbs	50g
Fried onion paste	1 cup	270g
Cashewnut paste	1 cup	250g
Coconut paste	1 cup	250g
Lemon juice	1 cup	240ml
Water	1 cup	240ml
Raisins	1 cup	140g
Coconut (grated)	1 cup	80g
Coconut (desiccated)	1 cup	55g

notes

notes